THREE PEAKS AND MALHAMDALE

*To know, to love and to cherish
and explore the countryside is
one of the surest ways to a
balanced spirit, to spiritual
renewal and physical well-being.*

Arthur Raistrick (1897-1991)
the Dales historian

THREE PEAKS AND MALHAMDALE

W R Mitchell

First published in 1992 by
Smith Settle Ltd
Ilkley Road
Otley
West Yorkshire
LS21 3JP

Reprinted 2002

ISBN 1 870071 85 9

British Library Cataloguing-in-Publication data:
A catalogue record for this book is available from the British Library.

Set in Monotype Ehrhardt

Designed, printed and bound by
SMITH SETTLE
Ilkley Road, Otley, West Yorkshire LS21 3JP

For Charlie Emett and Bill Bamlett, my companions
on many a walk in the Three Peaks Country.

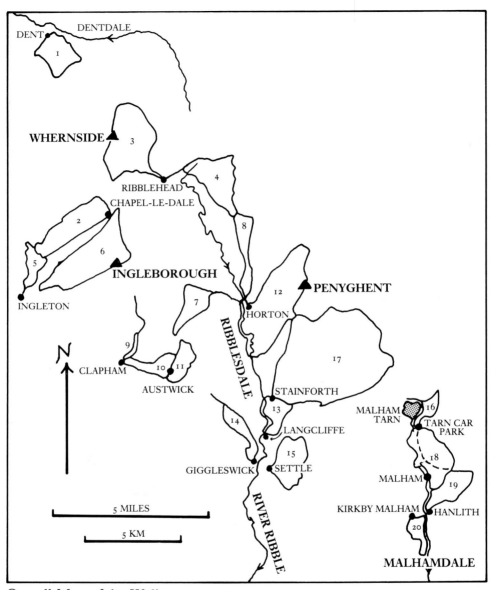

Overall Map of the Walks

CONTENTS

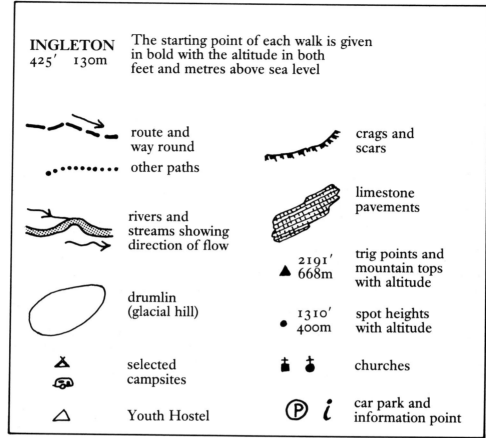

INGLETON
425′ 130m

The starting point of each walk is given in bold with the altitude in both feet and metres above sea level

route and way round

other paths

rivers and streams showing direction of flow

drumlin (glacial hill)

selected campsites

Youth Hostel

crags and scars

limestone pavements

▲ 2191′ 668m — trig points and mountain tops with altitude

• 1310′ 400m — spot heights with altitude

churches

ⓟ 𝒾 — car park and information point

Key to maps

INTRODUCTION

This new-style walker's guide, one of a series devised by Smith Settle, is useful and also companionable.

It offers ideas and brief directions for twenty attractive walks, mainly in classic limestone country. The text includes explanatory notes on the natural life and lore of the district – geology, history, birds, beasts and flowers. Clear maps and a variety of illustrations, some in colour, complement the text.

Here is a series of circular walks for which directions are minimal where paths are easy to follow. The walker, seeing objects as diverse as an unfamiliar flower, a limekiln, historic church or a major geological feature, is given background information in a handy form.

It is both a joy and a responsibility to undertake a guide to the Three Peaks and Malhamdale, an area of outstanding beauty and scientific interest about which perceptive visitors have been writing for some 200 years.

The Yorkshire Dales National Park footpath officer reassured me with regard to official rights of way. Naturalist friends scanned the passages relating to wildlife and flora. As I walked the routes, I thought of many fine potholers, fell-walkers and naturalists of the past who considerably enlarged my knowledge of the Three Peaks and Malhamdale by sharing their experiences.

Thanks are also due to Janet Rawlins, who has enhanced this book with her watercolours and line drawings of flora and fauna, and to David Leather, who drew the maps and geological sections, and also made helpful suggestions for the route to walk 17. The photographs are by the author, with additional colour photographs by Trevor Croucher and John Edenbrow. Peter Fox supplied the print of Ribblehead Viaduct.

A special word of thanks is due to Mark Whitley and the publishers Smith Settle, for their advice and help during the preparation of the book.

W R Mitchell
Giggleswick 1992

AUTHOR'S NOTE

Many of these walks are on limestone, which becomes slippery in wet weather. The Pennine weather is variable; sunshine may quickly be succeeded by shower. The fell tops are chilly places even in summer. Be well equipped for all hill outings. Wear durable boots and carry waterproof outer clothing and an extra jumper, and take a hot drink if possible.

Every effort has been made to ensure that the walks outlined in this book are on public rights of way. Please keep to the public footpaths and respect the countryside. The Yorkshire Dales National Park is not, as its name might suggest, an area that has been nationalised. Less than one per cent of the land is under public ownership.

In case of emergency, dial 999 or contact Settle Police Station (01729 822542), through which the Cave Rescue Organisation is alerted. The members, all volunteers, have the manpower and equipment to bring down injured people from the fells.

ACKNOWLEDGMENTS

Thanks are due to the following people for permission to reproduce the undermentioned illustrations:

Trevor Croucher, front cover, p104; John Edenbrow, p108; Peter Fox, p38; David Leather, pp2, 48, and all maps; Janet Rawlins, pp18, 19, 24, 25, 27, 34, 43, 59, 66, 73, 86, 95, 100, 105, 113, 118.

All other illustrations were provided by the author.

PUBLIC TRANSPORT

Arriva (formerly Northern Spirit) operates a Leeds–Carlisle service via Settle and Appleby to Carlisle, using Super Sprinters. Bus links from selected stations are shown on the printed timetable, which is available free of charge from local stations. A rail service is also available from Skipton to Carnforth (for Lancaster), stopping at Gargrave, Hellifield, Long Preston, Giggleswick and Clapham. (Train timetable enquiries: 0845 748 49 50.)

Pennine Motor Services of Gargrave (01756 749215) links Skipton with Settle and Malhamdale. Some buses go through to Ingleton. Tyrer Tours (01282 861234) connects Clitheroe with Settle. Kirkby Lonsdale Mini-Coaches (015242 72239) operates a service that takes in Horton-in-Ribblesdale, Settle, Austwick, Clapham and Ingleton. For timetables, see the booklet *Transport Times for Craven District*, available free of charge from the tourist information centres listed below.

TOURIST INFORMATION

Clapham, National Park Centre (015242 51419).
Horton-in-Ribblesdale, Tourist Information Centre, Penyghent Café (01729 860333).
Ingleton, Tourist Information Centre, Community Centre Car Park, Main Street (015242 41049).
Malham, National Park Centre (01729 830363).

ROCKS AND THE LANDSCAPE

Follow the zigzag route up the side of Castleberg, the limestone knoll dominating Settle Market Place like a piece of scenery in a Wagnerian opera. From the summit, your eyes take in a broad, sweet-and-sour countryside.

The sweetness is limestone, represented by creamy grey scars and steep fields with close-cropped verdant grass. The sourness is in the gritstone country to the west, where the shallow valley of the Ribble and smooth hills of Bowland form a darker landscape.

The geological fault which produced this dramatic contrast passes through the town of Settle, set out far below like a model on a planner's table.

This guidebook deals mainly with the limestone country, for which the Three Peaks and Malham, in the southern part of the Yorkshire Dales National Park, have long been celebrated. The limestone was fashioned by ice and water into cliffs and scars, clints and grikes, gorges, pavements, potholes and caves.

Whernside (2,414 ft/736m), Ingleborough (2,373 ft/723m) and Penyghent (2,273 ft/694m) are skirted by limestone pavements, and the head of Malhamdale impresses with its naked grey rock and springy, floriferous turf, about which Charles Kingsley wrote in the early chapters of *The Water-Babies*.

In Dentdale, which drains into the Dee, thin beds of limestone form 'steps' down which the river flows, though often the bed is dry and, as is the way in limestone country, the water goes underground to flow through 'measureless caverns'.

Limestone lights up a landscape, and quite often the sky tones are stronger than those of the land. Limestone is mostly light grey, but on a bright day in March the scars gleam bone-white against the blue-black of a passing storm cloud. Limestone, which looks rosy pink – even golden – in the rays of a setting sun, is livid under a thundery sky.

Carboniferous Sequence The Three Peaks are composed of a succession of rocks that lie almost level, one above another, like layers in a sponge cake. This is an uncomplicated landscape. All the visible rocks (except some outcrops in the Ingleton Glens and along the bottoms of the dales) are of the Carboniferous Age, between 360 and 290 million years old.

The rocks of the Carboniferous sequence represent sediments that accumulated in sea, swamp and delta over an immense period of time. Here and there are outstanding examples of an 'unconformity', where the Carboniferous sequence is seen resting on the much older rocks. It occurs at Foredale near Helwith Bridge, and also at Thornton Force in the glens of Ingleton (*walk 5*).

Great Scar Limestone Resting on its slaty bed, and dominating the scenery around Ingleton, Settle and Malham, the Great Scar limestone attains a thickness of over 600 feet (200m). Its marine origin is evident to anyone who studies the fossils, the skeletal remains of small sea creatures which abounded in a clear warm sea, bright with corals which now resemble petrified macaroni, and crinoids, also known as sea lilies from their long feathery arms.

Limestone, buried under other sedimentary rocks, was subjected to enormous pressures which broke and 'faulted' it. In geologically recent times, the overlying material was eroded to reveal the

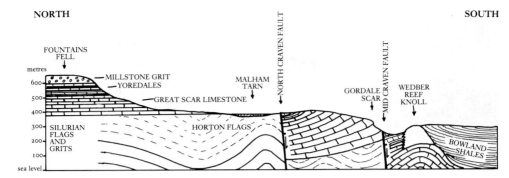

A section showing the geology from Fountains Fell to Wedber near Malham. The Craven Faults show a downward displacement of rocks to the south.

limestone in all the beauty of its smooth, pale forms. Pick up a piece of limestone and you may see the fossils of shells and corals, varying much in shape and size.

The Yoredales The Yoredale series, above the Great Scar limestone, takes its name from an old name for Wensleydale, where the geologist John Philips studied and named the rocks in 1833. The Yoredales, with a total thickness of some 1,000 feet (300m), consist of bands of limestone along with layers of shale and sandstone in a repeating succession. Because the various layers have differing degrees of resistance to erosion, the slopes are 'stepped', as on Penyghent when viewed from Horton-in-Ribblesdale (*walk 7*).

In the shale of the Yoredale series may be found thin, brittle seams of coal. The summit of Fountains Fell (*walk 17*) had its colliery for many years. A number of small coal pits and one large colliery were to be found in the Ingleton area. The coal seams lay south of the fault line, but originally were connected with seams (long since eroded) at the top of Ingleborough.

Millstone Grit Above the strata of the Yoredales is millstone grit, so named because its coarseness made it suitable for millstones; they did not overheat the grain. Gritstone, which is seen extensively to the east, is represented in the Three Peaks area as small impervious caps on the principal hills.

Faulting Limestone, made up almost entirely of calcium carbonate, is characterised by joints. These faults (vertical cracking) form a major feature of the earth's crust in the area covered by this guide. They have a drop of over 5,000 feet (1,500m) to the south, hence the contrast in scenery between the landscapes north and south of the fault line.

Where that fault line occurs, as with the South Craven Fault at Buckhaw Brow near Settle, there is a dramatic demarcation between limestone and millstone grit (*walk 14*). Those who travel by road up Buckhaw Brow see gritstone to the left and limestone scars as dominant features to the right.

The drystone walls are a good guide to the geology of the Dales, for no waller

The classic limestone landscape is typified by Scales Moor, with an erratic boulder, and Whernside in the background.

carried stone further than necessary! In the vicinity of Buckhaw Brow they are white, becoming mottled, then brown, as the fault line is crossed.

South of Malham Tarn (the bed of which is composed of impervious slate) is the North Craven Fault; the limestone that begins here ends dramatically less than two miles (3 km) away at Malham Cove (*walk 18*), which is on the Mid Craven Fault.

The Ice Age The landscapes we see today took their present form as the result of glaciation. What is popularly known as the Ice Age lasted for about 1,000,000 years and ended in geologically recent times – 13,000 to 14,000 years ago. At its maximum depth, the ice completely smothered the Dales area.

On to the old pattern of river valleys was imposed the sculpturing effect of an enormous weight of slow-moving ice, which transformed an old V-shaped river valley into one with a conspicuous U-shape, the sides of the valley being plastered with ground-up material called boulder clay.

Nonetheless, within the limestone context, the Dales have variety. Kingsdale is a somewhat secret valley, tucked away between Gragareth and Whernside. Glacial ice made deep incisions at Kingsdale and Chapel-le-Dale. There is a sense of mystery about little Clapdale (*walk 9*) and Crummackdale (*walk 7*).

Glacial features of special interest are the Norber erratics, on the hill of that name just north of Austwick (*walk 10*), where boulders of Silurian slate, broken by ice from their native beds in Crummackdale, were dumped on limestone at a higher elevation. Some boulders – by sheltering the limestone immediately beneath them – retarded the process of erosion and now stand on foot-high plinths.

North Ribblesdale, east of the river and to the south of Gearstones (*walk 4*), has a notable drumlin field, the many rounded green hills – created by glacial action and containing clay, pebbles and other debris – having a 'basket of eggs' appearance.

The Three Peaks area is famous for features created when the ice thawed after a long period of refrigeration. Meltwater flowing over frozen ground created gorges

Limestone pavements, like this one in the shadow of Ingleborough, were exposed by the scouring effect of Ice Age glaciers.

such as Gordale Scar, nearly 500 feet (150m) deep, at the head of Malhamdale (*walk 18*). The 240 feet (73m) high curved cliff of Malham Cove, which at one time was a tropical underwater cliff, had its final shaping through a flow of water in what is now a dry valley, the water pouring over the lip of the cliff in a waterfall as high as Niagara and eroding it backwards.

Where glacial ice scraped away the soil of the higher ground, limestone pavements appeared to view. Their distinctive appearance came about through the widening of joints (grikes) in the limestone by water solution, forming isolated blocks (clints). Broad clints and especially deep grikes lie to the north-west of Ingleborough. Of special interest is the dissected surface at the head of Malham Cove.

Many water- and weather-worn limestone rocks, sculptured into fantastic shapes, were to be removed for gardens. Today only a few thousand acres of limestone pavement remain in the country, and every effort is being made to discourage gardeners from using rockery stones from this source.

Potholes and Caves The Three Peaks are 'hollow mountains' in the sense that the Great Scar limestone is riddled with underground systems, some 600 of which are known. Water goes to ground at the Great Scar limestone and re-emerges above the impervious slate. In between is a honeycomb of potholes and caves, which have a stimulating variability to experienced people who explore them and who are usually known as potholers.

Conspicuous surface features are the hundreds of funnel-like depressions known by various names – such as shakehole, swallow hole or sinks. A widespread group of shakeholes occurs on the Ingleton side of the Ribblehead Viaduct (*walk 3*).

4

The characteristic 'stepped' profile of Penyghent (with Dale Head in the foreground) is due to the differing speeds of erosion of the Yoredale series of rocks.

The large open shafts, such as Gaping Gill and Alum Pot, are truly impressive – and should be approached with care. To the first tourists – those 'curious travellers' of the Romantic Age (1760-1820) – some caves were a special type of scenery, inspiring feelings of awe and dread.

Priscilla Wakefield was a member of a small party who entered the roofless Weathercote Cave in Chapel-le-Dale, 'where we were alarmed, not only by the increasing sound of the cascade, which became tremendous, but by the shaking of the rocks on which we stood, as well as those around us'. In 1808, the artist J M W Turner portrayed Weathercote, with its waterfall pouring from below a perched

rock known as Mahommet's Coffin, including in the spray the rainbow that appears when the summer sun slants down the shaft.

How the underworld of natural shafts and galleries was formed is a fascinating story. The top of the Great Scar limestone around Ingleborough lies on the 1,300 feet (400m) contour. Rainwater, which takes in carbon dioxide from the air and becomes a weak carbonic acid, seeps through the peaty soil and absorbs more acids. Having gained access to the limestone through fractured rock, it widens and opens up the cracks by dissolving them.

The main shaft of Gaping Gill (*walk 9*) receives Fell Beck, draining the eastern

5

Thornton Force – a classic example of a geological unconformity.

watercourses which form the headwaters of the River Aire, being mainly composed of water that went to ground at a sink in the vicinity of the smelt mill chimney, a prominent feature on Malham Moor. The Aire has its source at Aire Head, about half a mile below Malham village.

The dry upper passages of many caves are decked with calcite formations – stalactites and stalagmites (the 'mites' look up at the 'tites'). These formations are created by percolating water which redeposits the lime from solution. Formations might join to form pillars. The most delicate features are straw stalactites that respond to the slightest movements, even to vibrations from the human voice.

Specimens of the main types of formations caused by deposition from a flow of lime-laden water are to be seen at close quarters in White Scar Cave, near Ingleton, and at Ingleborough Cave, Clapham (*walk 13*). In the last-named system, a calcite formation resembles in shape one of the old straw skeps used for housing bees and is therefore called the Bee Hive.

The erosive effect of an active watercourse is evident in the 'forces' (waterfalls), of which there are many fine examples, one being Catrigg Force near Stainforth (*walk 13*). The cap of hard rock has endured longer than the soft strata beneath, and thus a stream descends in a series of splendid leaps. At Gordale Scar and Janet's Foss in Malhamdale (*walk 19*) may be seen a variation on the theme, with erosion followed by calcitic deposition on mosses, giving them a spongy texture, leading to the creation of a hard substance called tufa.

side of Ingleborough. This water tumbles into the shaft, creating one of the highest waterfalls in the land at 340 feet (103m). Alum Pot near Selside is 200 feet (60m) deep, a special feature being a huge displaced boulder which forms a natural bridge some 100 feet (30m) below the surface.

The beck emerging from the base of Malham Cove (*walk 18*) is one of three

So the geological process never stops.

MAN AND THE LANDSCAPE

Traces of human activity have been preserved for thousands of years in 'bone caves', especially those on the limestone scars to the east of Settle. They indicate that the first humans, who moved as insubstantial as shadows across a stark postglacial landscape, hunted and fished for food. One man's treasured double-barbed harpoon, fashioned from antler, lay among cave remains.

At Victoria Cave (*walk 15*), objects from two periods of human occupation have been found. The associated objects ranged from artefacts of Mesolithic times to a bronze dragonesque brooch bearing traces of enamel and dating from the Iron Age. There were also bones of post-glacial mammals like reindeer and Arctic fox.

Below these deposits was a thick layer of glacial clay, separating the comparatively modern remains from the bones of pre-Ice Age creatures such as woolly hippopotamus, slender-nosed rhinoceros and straight-tusked elephant, which doubtless roamed the district during a warm interglacial period. It may be that what is now known as Victoria Cave was then the den of hyena.

Such caves may have been bad-weather refuges for those early hunters or even used for rites associated with the dead. Bone caves have been found near Trow Gill above Clapham (*walk 9*) and at Kinsey Cave on Giggleswick Scar (*walk 14*). Amateur archaeologists, including William Kinsey Mattinson of Austwick, after whom Kinsey Cave was named, trenched a mass of rock debris at the base of a cliff and found a fragment of a worked rod or lancepoint made of reindeer-antler.

For 1,000 years and more, hunter-gatherers found good living conditions in areas of free-draining limestone, with its light covering of woodland composed mainly of ash, hazel and birch. In the valleys, by this time, birch and pine had been largely succeeded by oak, elm and alder.

A slash-and-burn technique, to create open ground, served the early peoples well. The Mesolithic period (8000-2500 BC) saw the beginnings of what was to be man's devastating mark on the landscape. The Great Cumbrian Axe, fashioned from an especially hard volcanic rock found in central Lakeland and traded over a wide area, was in skilful hands a formidable cutting implement in the woods.

The Neolithic folk (3000-1500 BC), who were the first real farmers, occupied houses made of wood on free-draining ground well above the marshy or densely-wooded valleys. It was almost certainly during this time that the Giant's Grave, at the head of Penyghent Gill, was used for the burial of a notable person. Bronze Age settlement (2000-600 BC) was not very extensive in the Craven district.

A Celtic culture arrived on the Craven uplands about 750 BC – very much later than elsewhere in the country. These Iron Age folk of Northern England became known as the Brigantes. A climate which had been cold and wet improved a good deal, making settlement on the hills tolerable.

The Brigantes were soon under pressure from the Romans, who arrived in the region in the first century AD. They controlled movement in the region, without actually conquering it, through a system of forts and good roads, one of which extended from Virosidum (Bainbridge) across Cam End to the head of Ribblesdale (*walk 2*) and traversed Chapel-le-Dale towards a fort at Burrow by the Lune.

A section of 'Celtic' wall near Feizor.

It may be that the Brigantean patriot Venutius had a hill fort on Ingleborough, where a gritstone wall was raised to form a rampart for a substantial defence system (*walk 6*). The 3,000 feet (915m) long wall, which enclosed some 15 acres (6 ha) of plateau, was originally 13 feet (4m) thick. In the event, the battle between the Brigantes and the Romans was fought at Stanwix, near what is now Barnard Castle. On Ingleborough, what Jacquetta Hawkes refers to as 'perhaps the most moving monument to pre-historic man in all Yorkshire' has suffered over the years from pilfering to make cairns and even, in the nineteenth century, a castellated hospice, commissioned by a new lord of the manor and vandalised by drunken workers on the opening day!

Some of the so-called 'Celtic fields' are seen to good effect at Malham (*walk 18*). They are what survives of early efforts to enclose land for cultivation and are usually in rectangular plots. The associated lynchets are evident in many places, including Settle, Austwick and Clapham. These terraces were created gradually through the shifting of soil down the slope when ploughing a hillside in one direction. Many old field boundaries were obliterated when the landscape was overlaid with drystone walls during the enclosure period of the eighteenth and early nineteenth centuries.

Craven, the name for a district now recalled by an archdeaconry, is one of the few remaining Celtic names, derived from 'land of crags', though some claim it to be 'the land of wild garlic'. To the Celts, a hill was *penno*, hence Penyghent, and the name Crummack, a small dale near Austwick, relates to its stream or beck.

The Dales country was settled by immigrants from the Continent – by Angles (well established by the middle of the seventh century) and later by Danes. These settlers were content to inhabit their *hams* and *tuns*, as their farms were known, in the lower dales. The name Ribble, for the river, is said to be Old English (possibly from *ripel*, indicating a boundary).

The last major settlement was the arrival, early in the tenth century, of the Irish-Norse folk. They spread themselves out thinly at the daleheads and on higher ground, to such good effect that Norse names became the language of topography, some names supplanting those given by earlier peoples. The map is liberally sprinkled with Norse terms: fell, dale, beck, clint, crag, gill, rigg, moss, scar and tarn.

What is thought to have been a Norse farm of 1,100 years ago was excavated in an area of limestone pavement near Ribblehead. The house, some sixty feet (18m) long, consisted of a low stone wall and high thatched roof. The remains of two smaller buildings were found, along with low but stockproof walls.

From this time, the incessant grazing of many sheep inhibited the natural regeneration of timber, giving the landscape its bare appearance and ribbing the hills with narrow tracks. For 1,000 years the district has had the reek of sheep. A walker who sees a tree on the fells may be sure it is growing from the side of a rocky gill or from a pothole and is beyond reach of the sheep. In many areas, the coverlet of ling (the commonest of our heathers) has been grazed off, leaving a landscape of coarse unpalatable grasses.

Following the Norman Conquest, and William's savage reprisals against rebel-lious Northern folk, much of the land was rendered 'waste'. Daleheads were now set aside for hunting by the nobility. In North Ribblesdale, the *Domesday* scribes went only as far as Stainforth; beyond here there was nothing special to note.

Some upland areas were in due course granted to the monasteries. Having territorial interests in High Craven were Fountains, Furness, Sawley, Jervaulx and Byland Abbeys. The first named is perpetuated in the Three Peaks country by the placename Fountains Fell (*walk 17*). At Dale Head, formerly at the roadside but now just over a wall, lies the base of the old Ulfkil Cross, one of the monastic boundary stones.

Through their extensive interest in wool, the monks managed to serve both God and Mammon. The Cistercians were noted for keeping sheep. At Fountains Abbey, in the valley of the Skell near Ripon, the monks were wealthy landowners whose interests extended to the heart of the Lake District. Sheep kept on Fountains Fell were driven to the monastic grange at Kilnsey in Wharfedale for washing and clipping. The wool was transported by ox-hauled wains to Fountains, where it was stored. Much of the wool was sold to foreign merchants and exported to the Continent.

What is now Ingman Lodge in North Ribblesdale and the hall at Newby, near Clapham, were granges (outliers) of Furness Abbey. A grange had its living quarters, chapel and farm. The outer grazings would be located at Newby Head, on the watershed between Ribblehead and Hawes.

Jervaulx ('Ure-valley'), having been granted land in North Ribblesdale, bred horses at what is now Studfold, a settlement near Helwith Bridge (*walk 12*). Stained glass at Horton-in-Ribblesdale Church (*walk 7*) includes a representation of the mitred head of Thomas à Becket.

Seventeenth century Dales architecture: Friars Head, Winterburn.

These fragments of glass may have been moved from Jervaulx Abbey to Horton at the Dissolution in the sixteenth century.

A desperate need for farmland, especially during the Middle Ages, led to further cultivation of the hillsides; by following the contours, this created more strip lynchets, those terraces caused by the movement of earth through regular ploughing.

Stone-and-slate farmhouses of the seventeenth century express, by their dignified but unpretentious appearance, the yeoman spirit that was evident when feudalism came to an end. An early stone building of this new age is Friars Head, Winterburn, a three-storeyed structure with tripartite windows and decked by finials. It can be seen at the roadside between Eshton and Winterburn.

Ingman Lodge, the former grange of Furness near Ribblehead (*Three Peaks Walk*), is also three-storeyed, its elaborate doorway being adorned on each side by a representation of a halberd. Hill Top, at Malham, which has the date 1617 above the main door, maintains the vernacular style with its stone-mullioned windows and gabled porch.

Visitors at the time of the Enclosure Acts

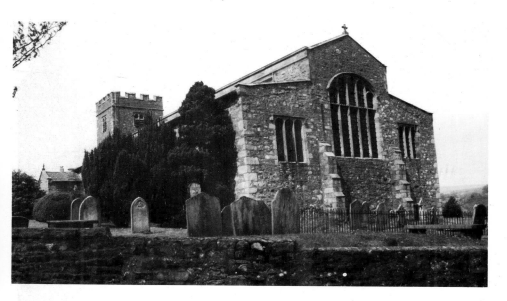

A church was first built at Dent in the twelfth century, and the Early English north doorway still remains in the present building.

commented with amazement on the 'gridiron' pattern of the new drystone walls. Land had been enclosed, using 'dry' stones, from early times. The majority of the Parliamentary enclosures were carried out between 1760 and 1830.

Behind the walls, the land use could be regulated and the ground improved – as with the use of lime, burnt before spreading in the many field kilns. These were built near limestone outcrops and within carting distance of supplies of brittle but burnable coal from seams in the Yoredale rocks.

The type of wall to be constructed was specified by the Enclosure Acts. It was to be, in effect, two walls in one, bound together by large stones called throughs, and with fillings for the remaining spaces and capstones to reinforce the top. In North Ribblesdale, many throughs are pieces of Horton flagstone, quarried near Helwith Bridge (*walk 12*).

With the walls came many of the field barns and other evidence of the pastoral farming which is a feature of the Dales to this day, though on a diminishing scale. The number of people engaged in farming has declined with mechanisation.

Industrial development in the eighteenth century took the form of cotton mills, using waterpower. Notable among them is High Mill at Langcliffe, one of very few remaining Arkwright mills, now owned by a firm of paper manufacturers (*walk 14*).

Quarrying for limestone in North Ribblesdale assumed its large-scale commercial aspects when the railways arrived, firstly the 'Little' North Western Railway northwards from Skipton (1847), and subsequently the Settle-Carlisle

The Swaledale breed of sheep.

(1876) which used the two major north-south valleys of the Ribble and Eden and connected the two over the high Pennines with viaducts, tunnels and ledges cut from bare hillsides.

Today, limestone is transported noisily and dustily across country and through towns and villages by heavy lorries, and the railways are considerably under-used. No longer is the limestone burnt locally. A Hoffman-type limekiln (for continuous burning) that was installed at Ingleton (*walk 5*) and, in a larger form, at Craven Quarry, Langcliffe (*walk 13*), are studied by industrial archaeologists. They have not been used for many years, being labour intensive and therefore costly as wage rates improved.

Farming of a pastoral kind, practised for well over 1,000 years, has helped to shape the landscape as we see it today. The hill ewe (often referred to as 'yow'), being able to thrive on coarse vegetation growing on bleak hills, enables the farmer to obtain a cash-crop from unpromising land. The dales are devoted to permanent grassland, from which hay or silage is taken, and rough grazing for the large stocks of horned sheep and cattle of mixed breed being raised as 'sucklers' for beef production.

The true hill farms, with little or no valley-bottom land, include Penyghent House and Rainscar, beside the Stainforth-Halton Gill road, from which there is a splendid view of 't'back o' Penyghent'. At such an upland sheep farm, where there might be 1,000 sheep ranging over 3,000 acres, much depends economically on the availability of family labour.

The Dales farmer plays a traditional role in the landscape, needing judgement and skill in the management of his stock and the use of the 'fell' and 'inland'. Like his ancestors, he must know his sheep as individuals. Haytime is now rarely seen. The farmer, with few helpers but several ingenious machines, quickly ensiles grass, keeping it in large plastic bags. He rounds up his sheep riding a tricycle with 'balloon' tyres, taking his sheepdog as a pillion passenger.

The sheep of the high hills are the Swaledales (with a dark face and grey nose) or Dalesbred (also dark-faced, but with white marks on either side of the nostril). In lower Dentdale, the sheep are Rough Fell (a dark pattern on white).

The ewes give birth to their lambs in fields handy to the farm buildings, and the farmers then drive them back on to the hills. In early summer, there may be over 500,000 ewes and lambs in the area of the Yorkshire Dales National Park. Many are sold at the autumnal sales, so that the winter population of sheep is much smaller.

Years ago, the dual-purpose (milk/beef) Shorthorn cow was kept, and spare milk was converted into butter and cheese. Now, milk production is absent at most of the dalehead farms and 'sucklers' (cross-bred beef cattle with calves at foot) are the rule.

In lower country, the black-and-white Friesian is extensively used for milk production.

The traditional hill farmer, now in straitened circumstances, has nonetheless a vital role in conserving the Dales scenery, its wildlife and flora. He must be encouraged by all who enjoy the Dales landscape. Gone are most of the old-time 'flower meadows'. The owners of those that remain are encouraged by subsidy to mow them after a specific date, when the plants have set seed, and not to add artificial fertilisers. The low ground, ploughed and re-seeded with commercial strains of grass, has become uniformly green.

Mass tourism, which had its beginnings in Victorian times with the coming of the railways and cheap excursions from the large towns to places like Settle and Ingleton, is mainly car-based. With walking as a major national pastime, car parks at Ingleton, Horton, Settle and Malham are well used throughout the year.

What does the future hold? There will undoubtedly be fewer farms. The high sheep population will be reduced. More of the hill country will be planted with conifers. A larger proportion of houses will be occupied by retired people. Tourism will dominate local life, with more and more unsightly surfaced footpaths and car parks. Theme parks, with toilets and tea shops, will cater for those interested in the traditional local life.

WILDLIFE

John Ruskin, the eminent Victorian, when travelling through Chapel-le-Dale on a windy day, looked at the steep face of Ingleborough and wondered how the hill managed to stand without rocking. The Three Peaks country can be wild, even rugged in places.

Wildlife is as diverse and numerous as conditions of food and sanctuary allow. The uplands, either the limestone pavements or peaty moor, have relatively few wild species, though almost every view includes the commonest mammal of all – the sheep.

The district has a few natural woods. On Oxenber, near Austwick, an old-style wood has survived because only fallen timber has been removed. The local mix of trees grows from grikes (cracks) in limestone. A scattering of trees clings to the steep ground at Cave Ha', just north of Buckhaw Brow, and this woodland can be readily seen from a road layby.

Mixed and coniferous woodland, of the type favoured by old estates, is evident at the glens of Ingleton, in Clapdale near Clapham and at Malham Tarn. The largest tract of commercial forest is Greenfield, to the north of Penyghent.

Malham Tarn (walk 16) is exceptional, being one of only two large natural tarns in the Dales and having an elevation of over 1,000 feet (300m). The nesting birds include the great crested grebe, a water bird which dons chestnut and black head frills for the nesting season and usually builds a floating nest, tethered to waterside vegetation. At Malham Tarn, the water is frequently stirred by high winds.

Much smaller tarns on Whernside and Fountains Fell are frequented by waterfowl in transit. There is often a chance of seeing two upland waders: the golden plover, once known as the 'Pennine whistler', its dark mantle spotted with gold and with dark underparts; and the dunlin, also known as 'the plover's page', looking like a small version, though not related.

In winter, when the Ribble overflows, considerable stretches of floodwater in the valley between Settle and Long Preston attract waterfowl. Rivers and becks, with their attendant trees, provide food and sanctuary for wildlife. Old quarries, now overgrown, have become unofficial wildlife sanctuaries. (They are also privately owned.) Railways that include the celebrated Settle-Carlisle line are, in effect, linear nature reserves.

Mammals Roe deer have recently colonised the area from Lakeland, infiltrating the valleys of Lune, Wenning and Greta, with others arriving from the North-East via the Dales. This relatively small deer, fox-red in summer and greyer in winter, has short branched antlers (worn by the buck), a kidney-shaped patch of white hair at the rump and a gruff call when disturbed. Roe are now in most suitable tracts of woodland around the Peaks and also in the woodland at Malham Tarn (walk 16).

Feral sika deer, of the Japanese sub-species, now well-established in Bowland, are sometimes seen as far east as the A65. These are medium-sized deer, with coats of dappled chestnut in summer and grey-brown in winter. The antlers of the stags are branched, as with the red deer. The caudal disc (or rump patch) is large and white. When alarmed, the sika gives a short high-pitched squeal.

The badger, 'our little English bear', with its boldly-striped head and low-slung

The golden plover has a gold-flecked back and white-bordered black breast.

body, is unlikely to be seen in the open by day, though in quiet areas it leaves its sett an hour or so before the light fades. Elsewhere, it appears at dusk. Most badgers have their setts in woodland.

The fox is infrequently seen in daylight. The otter is so uncommon that if what appears to be one is observed, it is more likely to be a mink, descendant of an escapee from a fur farm. Stoats and weasels, small and lithesome mammals, are usually well concealed in thick vegetation but occasionally announce their presence by a swift dash across a road. The stoat has a black tip to its tail.

Grey squirrels have occupied the wooded areas; they are regularly seen in the Settle area, the species having spread from Bowland. A likely place to view a grey squirrel is near the wooden cafe in the glen below Thornton Force, Ingleton (*walk 7*). Hares are less common than they were. A walker who sees one spring from a nearby lie should look for the form (daytime resting place), where the hare's body has flattened the grass; it may still be warm to the touch.

Fish Malham Tarn's stock of trout was the basis of a valuable fishery in monastic times. Charles Kingsley, when a guest of Walter Morrison of Malham Tarn, described the fishing as 'the best in the whole earth'. On the 5th July 1858, he wrote of the tarn:

'My largest fish to-day (a cold North Wester) was 1½ lb., but with a real day I could kill 50 lb. Unfortunately, it wants all my big lake flies which I, never expecting such a treat, left at home.'

The National Trust allow fishing from a boat by permit.

Brown trout inhabit the River Ribble, along with eels and crayfish, the latter being the 'freshwater lobster' and renowned for the delicate taste of its flesh.

Migratory fish, including salmon, travel to the headwaters of the Ribble to spawn. Concrete 'ladders' (a series of artificial pools) enable the fish to negotiate the weirs at Settle and Langcliffe. When the salmon are 'running' in late summer, the best place to see them is Stainforth Force (*walk 13*).

Butterflies and Moths A few resident species of butterfly are found on the grassier areas at low altitude where, in early summer, you might see the widely distributed small heath. The green-veined white occurs in moist woody areas and on marshy grassland. In an area of limestone grassland, the common blue flies from mid-May to mid-June. This species is double-brooded, and a few may be seen at the end of August and into September.

In upland areas, up to 100 species of moth fly at night in areas where the herbage is tall and the flora varied. If an area is heavily grazed, the moth population is small. Research into the species and their lifestyle is continuing.

A walker in an area where heather is common might look out for some of the more showy caterpillars – the rich dark brown and very hairy body of the three inch (7½ cm) long fox moth and, roughly similar in appearance, though banded with paler yellow, the northern eggar. Occasionally, the bright apple-green caterpillar of the emperor moth may be seen.

Birds Rudyard Kipling, famous for his Indian stories, had family connections with Yorkshire and knew the Dale country well. In one of his tales, he placed his famous soldier trio on a Himalayan ridge, with kites in view, and then arranged for Otheris to recall his native Pennines:

'Moors an' moors an' moors, wi' never a tree for shelter, an' grey houses wi' flagstone rooves, and peewits cryin', and a windhover [kestrel] going to and fro just like these kites.'

No true wilderness exists in the Three Peaks countryside, but much of the area is high-lying and has a wilderness feel to it. The birdlife is diverse because the dales and gills (water-carved valleys on fellsides) extend lowland conditions to quite high elevations.

The district offers constant surprises, such as the nesting of house martins under the eaves of station buildings at Dent, 1,110 feet (335m) above sea level. This species also nests against overhangs at the huge natural cliff of Malham Cove.

Its old name of windhover perfectly describes the kestrel's characteristic posture over its hunting grounds.

Some Typical Bird Habitats:

Moors and Fells Swifts, with nests on old buildings in the towns and villages, hawk insects over the highest ground. These small, sooty-looking birds cut cleanly through the air on narrow, scythe-shaped wings.

In spring, a birdwatcher has a bonus if a 'trip' of dotterel is seen having a feeding break high on Ingleborough (*walk 6*) during a northward migratory journey. So confiding is the dotterel that there is time to take in some of the fine points of the

16

plumage – white eye-stripe, white chest-band, chestnut underparts, and black on its crown and belly.

Snow buntings, refugees from a distant northern winter, dance in the air like snowflakes as the wind carries them to the next patch of purple moor-grass, on the seeds of which they are feeding.

The most widely distributed and commonest nesting species on the hills is the meadow pipit, a small streaky-brown bird which may startle you as it flutters from its nest in a tuft of coarse grass just a few yards ahead of your feet. The song flight is distinctive, with the pipit descending with stiffened wings and tail, looking like a shuttlecock.

Where the ground is high and the vegetation sparse, as on Whernside or Fountains Fell (*walks 3 and 17*), the golden plover slips from its saucer-like nest, which is lined with grass and lichen, and does not reveal itself until it is well clear. The bird, perched on the edge of a peat hag, gives a succession of soulful whistles. The mantle of the plover is dark, spangled with gold. The bird moves with mincing steps.

A dunlin, which looks like a smaller version of the golden plover, prefers high ground with good cover close to a tarn. The first glimpse may be of the bird feeding at a tarnside. The trill of a dunlin from high in the air on a calm spring evening is one of the most enchanting of bird sounds.

The characteristic sound of moorland, such as that seen beside the Ribblehead-Newby Head road (*walk 4*) is the crowing of the red grouse – 'kowa, kowa, kowa' – uttered during the breeding season. The red grouse, which is most active early and late in the day, has a reddish-brown plumage and carries red wattles on its head, but you may have to be content to see the silhouette of an erect, alert and aggressively vocal bird breaking the nearest skyline as it keeps you under scrutiny. A car parked beside the road on open moorland makes a good hide for grouse-watching.

A declining number of black grouse frequent 'white' ground (coarse grassland as opposed to 'black', which is peaty moorland). The cock bird was once described to me as 'big as a littleish turkey'; the smaller female is known as greyhen, after the lighter tones of its plumage.

A carrion crow, glossy black with a heavy black bill, nests when possible in an isolated tree, lagging the large twiggy nest with sheep wool. (I once found a crow nest on a wall-top in Stockdale, above Settle, where trees are scarce.) Dales farmers detest crows, which may attack weakly or ailing lambs in spring. Crows (and foxes) are major predators on the eggs and young of ground-nesting birds.

The short-eared owl, a brownish bird with long wings, hunts voles and other small mammals by day, and rears its young in a nest made among the rushes. It has a curious flight display in spring, clapping its wings several times in rapid succession beneath its body.

The snipe, a long-billed bird, darts from the ground with an alarm sound that is similar to a sneeze and zig-zags evasively as it moves away. The agitated long-billed bird you may see on the capstone of a wall is named after its conspicuous legs – redshank.

Crags and Gills The peregrine falcon, its numbers now happily restored after being greatly reduced by agricultural poisons and egg collectors, is most often seen in flight, when its trim figure, long pointed wings angled slightly backwards, and slightly tapering tail help to clinch the identification. In the nesting season, its excited, high-pitched chattering draws attention to where it is discouraging an intruder in its air space, or giving flying lessons to its new-fledged young.

The grey wagtail favours fast-flowing stretches of water.

One or more pairs of ravens nest in the district, and some ravens from the northern Pennines winter here. Ravens nest early; they are patching up an old nest in February and attending their young by early April, just as the hill sheep are lambing, ensuring a plentiful supply of carrion as food. Large and glossy black, the raven draws attention to itself by its hoarse croaking and habit of flicking on to its back and flying upside down for a while. Jackdaws, gregarious birds with sharp, metallic calls, nest in cracks and crannies on some old quarry faces, and also at Gordale (*walk 18*).

In moorland gills where there is heather and running water (*walk 4*), look for the ring ouzel, which resembles a blackbird except that it carries a large white crescent across its breast. The female is lighter in hue than the male.

The lively dipper, small, dark and plump, bobs on a stone in the beck before plunging into the water to collect larvae. In the shallows, its back is in view as it seeks food. Sometimes it swims, looking as buoyant as a cork. Dippers are relatively common on the unpolluted streams and rivers of this area.

The grey wagtail, which is often found in the same habitat as the dipper, has blue-grey upperparts that contrast with the bright yellow of the breast. The nest of a grey wagtail is usually tucked away in a hole in the bank. The pied wagtail is not especially a streamside bird; it is frequently observed on the capstones of walls, in the hollow spaces of which it likes to nest.

The white-fronted dipper is able to walk along a river bottom in the search for food.

Deciduous Woodland Well-timbered areas, with some dead wood full of grubs, appeal to the green woodpecker, a bird also known as the yaffle after its laughing call (*walks 14 and 15*). It is a shy bird, but the resounding call gives away its presence.

Deciduous woods which are not too dense are the nesting place of woodcock (*walk 9*). The nest of this long-billed bird is a shallow depression in leaf-litter. Bird and eggs harmonise tonally with their surroundings, but the cock bird advertises itself at dusk as it flies round the perimeter of its territory, giving 'three grunts and a squeak' at intervals. This flight is known as 'roding'.

In well-wooded areas, the 'pink' of the chaffinch and the sweet song of the willow warbler are commonly heard. The tree-creeper, a mouse-like bird, moves in short bursts up the trunk of a tree, probing crannies with a thin decurved bill for insect food. The redstart, selecting lightly wooded areas in which to nest, calls sweetly and constantly flicks its rust-toned tail.

Pastures and Meadows The cock lapwing, with tufty wings and a jaunty head crest, tumbles in the air after giving an exuberant call, from which its alternative name of tewit is derived. The curlew, large and streaky-brown, with a long decurved bill and a bubbling trill, is instantly recognised, and for many visitors is the most memorable of the Pennine bird calls, though it does become a yelp if a walker accidentally goes too near a nest when the young have hatched.

Walls and rock outcrops offer nesting places for wheatears, which play hide-and-seek to deceive intruders (*walk 7*). The wheatear is small and lively, with a white rump and a hard 'chacking' call.

By the River A walk by the Ribble, between Settle and Stainforth (*walk 13*), introduces most of the birds of this habitat – the dipper, grey wagtail, mallard and perhaps a heron. A kingfisher might be seen as it flies fast and displays its back of ultramarine. On this stretch of river, I watched an angry kingfisher displaying to a 'rival', which was a small piece of blue fertiliser sack caught up in a riverside shrub during a spate. The red-breasted merganser, which now nests in the valley, choosing a hole by the riverbank, has a dark head sporting a double crest and a slender red bill with saw-like edges to retain slippery fish.

Around the head of Ribblesdale (*walk 4*), oystercatchers – large pied birds with long reddish bills and flesh-pink legs – nest on shingle. Sand martins, as dusky looking as their haunts, are less common than they were, but small numbers still excavate their nesting burrows in sandy banks.

Winter birdwatching in the Ribble Valley between Settle and Long Preston can be stimulating when the river has spilled over the earthbanks and flooded the water-meadows. Parties of wigeon feed in the shallows, the drakes announcing themselves with a double-syllable whistle – 'whee-oo'.

Some of the 400 Canada geese frequenting Stocks Reservoir, to the west, commute to the Ribble Valley. October usually brings a small herd of Icelandic whooper swans and, maybe, a few Bewicks swans, which are smaller, nesting much further north than their cousins.

A trumpeting chorus from swans in flight gives back to the Three Peaks area something of its old wilderness character.

FLORA

The Yorkshire limestone country has been a classic ground for botanists since John Ray, of Cambridge, explored and described its plant life around 1677. For example, he saw the alpine bistort 'in a mountainous pasture about a mile and a half from Wharfe', also noting the birdseye primrose, which still grows in that area.

A modern botanist, Geoffrey Grigson, in a pen portrait of Ingleborough, referred to its floral wealth. Here he found a 'wild garden of streams and natural sculpture and flowers'.

Visiting naturalists enthuse over the unique botanical world of the grikes (cracks) in limestone pavements – a community of plants akin to the old woodland vegetation, but surviving here because the flanking limestone blocks keep the plants shaded and moist.

Where limestone lies exposed in the Yoredale rocks of Penyghent and Ingleborough, a few alpines survive, the most showy of them being the purple saxifrage, which grows from rock crevices and produces its rose-purple flowers in late March.

On high ground where peat and heather occur, the cloudberry fruits in mid-July, the berry turning yellow when ripe. In Ling Gill and other rocky gorges at the head of Ribblesdale (*walk 4*), survivors from the ancient woodland – mountain ash, bird cherry and guelder rose – cling tenaciously to the cliffs and banks.

It has been argued that plant life is most varied where it is out of reach of sheep, which over the past 700 years have reduced the ground vegetation in general to something approaching a lawn. Yet on limestone pastures, where the dominant grass is named sheep's fescue, grazing is necessary to maintain the floral diversity.

In spring, the marsh marigolds (or kingcups) add a patch of yellow to moist places. A riverside stroll between Settle and Stainforth (*walk 13*) reveals woods with carpets of what wildflower books refer to as ramsons but most people know as wild garlic. Banks studded with primroses are in due course misty with bluebells.

Elsewhere, the spikes of the early purple orchid stand out prominently against short turf and creamy limestone. The strong stems of globe flowers support globes which have a lemon hue. Dorothy Wordsworth, who is most usually associated with the Lake District, was no stranger to the Dales. She wrote of the globe flower as 'a beautiful yellow, palish yellow, flower that looked thick, round, and double, and smelt very sweet – I supposed it was a ranunculus'.

The birdseye or mealy primrose – a favourite of Reginald Farrer, botanist, writer and flower painter, who was reared at Ingleborough Hall, Clapham – produces between May and early July an umbel of up to a dozen lilac-pink flowers (each with a yellow 'eye') on a slender stem which looks dusty towards the top and on the lower surface of the leaf. The yellow form of the mountain pansy is most common in the Craven district, though its distribution is patchy. Wild thyme imparts a fragrance to the summer landscape.

Now that road verges are not mown until the plants have set seeds, they are luxuriant, the display including the frothy white of meadowsweet. Sweet cicely, with its aniseed tang, cow parsley (Queen Anne's lace) and the purple-blue flowers of meadow cranesbill enliven the road verges.

The walker is aware of the change from limestone to gritstone by the increasing

Columbines in a woodland setting near Austwick.

drag on the boots! Damp, acidic ground, with coarse grasses and rush-bobs (as the Dales farmer calls the tufts of rushes), can be heavy going. You need not have crossed a geological fault, for pockets of glacial drift overlay the limestone.

Heather ground is not extensive in the Three Peaks area, where coarse, unpalatable mat-grass and purple moor-grass fill many a view. Heather moorland exists as such because the rank heather is swiddened (methodically fired in strips) in early spring to encourage the growth of new shoots, the food for sheep and grouse.

The Malham district has been studied in great detail at the field centre based at Malham Tarn House (*walk 16*). English Nature, formerly the Nature Conservancy Council, has a number of reserves, including Colt Park and Ling Gill in North Ribblesdale, where they now have a resident warden.

The Yorkshire Wildlife Trust maintains an important reserve at Southerscales in Chapel-le-Dale, where a public footpath follows firm ground over the limestone. The trust's Globe Flower Wood (which a local farmer's wife calls 'poppy wood') is at the junction of roads just east of Capon Hall on Malham Moor. This reserve need never be entered. It is enough, in springtime, simply to look over the wall.

Do not neglect garden walls in some of the old villages, where grow wall lettuce, wall rue, maidenhair spleenwort and rue-leaved saxifrage.

Some Typical Flower Habitats:

Most of the Pennine landscape is man-made in the sense that humans have tampered with the natural scene. Unwelcome changes are continuing, and in recent years, through ploughing and re-seeding, most of the 'flower fields' of the Dales country have been succeeded by limited strains of grasses suitable for making silage.

Many a tract of heather moor has had its character changed by over-grazing with sheep. Other areas have been blotted out by coniferous plantations.

Acid Moorland and Acid Bog (Peat Moss) Such moorland is to be found on the flanks of the Three Peaks, at Blea Moor and on ground adjacent to Malham Tarn. It has varying conditions, from dry ridges to ill-drained 'mosses' (bogs), which are particularly extensive on Whernside. A diverse plant life ranges from heather to sphagnum, from heath rush to soft rush.

Tormentil, with its four-petalled flowers, is widespread on the acid soils. Purple moor-grass is deciduous, losing its leaves in autumn; these leaves are blown away by the wind, hence its other name of flying bent.

Except where the wind has eroded the peat hags, the plant cover is virtually complete, with a russet and green mixture of heathers, predominantly ling. The wet, acidic soils hold cloudberry, crowberry and bilberry. There are also two insectivorous plants: round-leaved sundew, with leaves lying flat, covered in glandular hairs which secrete glistening droplets of liquid on which insects are trapped; and common butterwort, with leaves forming a rosette like a pale green starfish and clothed with sticky glands. These two plants obtain sustenance from their captives.

Cotton-grass sedges take their name from the fruiting head, which has white

Cotton-grass flowers as early as February.

cottony hairs. At its flowering stage, as early as February, it is known to the Dales farmer as moss-crop, providing an 'early bite' for hill sheep.

Limestone Cliffs Mention has been made of the purple saxifrage. Juniper, an evergreen clinging to limestone cliffs or forming a miniature woodland on limestone pavement, is not common in the Three Peaks country: its ability to resist wind means that it can grow at exposed sites. Juniper is to be seen at Gordale Scar (*walk 18*), on Moughton (*walk 11*) and on Giggleswick Scar (*walk 14*). The berries of this plant take two or three years to ripen;

The red-leaved herb robert is found in limestone pavements.

of the old natural woodland of the Pennines), wood anemone, herb robert (with bright pink flowers and a strong smell), and also many large ferns such as the broad and fleshy hart's tongue fern.

On the limestone rocks may grow smaller ferns, including wall rue, maidenhair spleenwort and the local green spleenwort, which has a green midrib.

Limestone Grassland   A great variety of grassland is found in the Three Peaks. A broad division is that between pastureland (which is grazed) and meadow (which, after being grazed, is left without stock for the vital month or so leading up to haytime).

On pastureland, the short, springy limestone turf overlies a shallow soil. Although in limestone country, the turf may be lime-deficient and also infertile because the high rainfall has leached out the nutrients. This infertility restricts the growth of coarse competitive grasses. As mentioned, sheep grazing keeps the turf short, also reducing competition and allowing a great variety of flowering plants to flourish.

Of the sweet limestone grasses, sheep's fescue, sweet vernal grass and crested dog's tail are important to stock. So is the blue moor-grass which, with blueish-purple flower buds, is one of the first grasses to grow in spring, providing an 'early bite' for the sheep.

The harebell, a mid-blue 'bell' on a slender stem, with the bell nodding in a breath of wind, is numerous near Malham. The diminutive plants of the limestone pastures are the aromatic thyme, eyebright (which seems to sparkle and was once used in the preparation of an eye tonic), and fairy flax (which is well-named, the tiny white flowers hanging on slender stalks).

Where there is unimproved grassland, the herb-rich vegetation includes a good spread of cowslips, though these are much

so you can expect to find blue and green berries, representing the fruit of two seasons, together.

Limestone Pavement   Limestone pavement, well seen on the skirts of Ingleborough and on Scales Moor between Chapel-le-Dale and Kingsdale (*walk 2*), appears at first glance to be a desert of grey stone, with the occasional hawthorn leaning in the direction of the prevailing wind.

Some pavements have colonies of lichen. Less evident until one looks closely are traces of an old woodland flora growing in the grikes. The plant species include dog's mercury, the delicate wood sorrel with leaves like those of clover (said to be a relic

Eyebright was formerly used to prepare an eye tonic.

scarcer than they were even thirty years ago.

Ash Wood on Limestone Permission to enter some ash woods in the Ingleborough area must be obtained from English Nature. At Colt Park, beware of the deep grikes. Here are hart's tongue fern, carpets of lily of the valley (with a much less pungent smell than ramsons, a wild garlic which has rather similar leaves) and dog's mercury.

The tree species at Colt Park, apart from the dominant ash, include the good old Dales mixture – birch, hazel, bird cherry, rowan, guelder rose, hawthorn and elder.

Needless to say, wild flowers should be looked at, not picked. It is illegal to pick most of them; and if collected, they would not survive a journey home.

WALK 1: DENT TOWN, FLINTERGILL AND THE DEE

Start: Dent Car Park. Grid Ref: 705 870
Distance: Rather more than 5 miles (8 km)
OS Map: Outdoor Leisure 2
Walking Time: 3 hours

Dentdale, a narrow valley with hedge-bordered roads, is bounded on the north by Rise Hill, known as the 'sunny side' as opposed to the 'money side', where the better land lies. Dent Town, the meeting place of three roads, has an eighteenth century atmosphere with its whitewashed buildings and cobbled streets, This walk, apart from an initial stiffish climb on a firm track, is on level ground or downhill, the last mile or two following a riverside path. Dent is reached from Ingleton on the B6255 (leave this road near Newby Head) or from Sedbergh (A683). There is a (pay) car park.

A slab of pink granite at the side of the cobbled street at Dent Town commemorates Adam Sedgwick (1785-1873), born in the parsonage and a pupil of Dent Grammar School, who became Woodwardian Professor of Geology at Cambridge and was one of the founders of the science of geology.

Hartley Coleridge described the street early last century:

'There is a town of little note or praise:
Narrow and winding are its rattling streets,
Where cart with cart in cumbrous conflict meets. . .'

The nearby church, a successor to the first modest building which served as a chapel to Sedbergh, is under the patronage of St Andrew and contains attractive Jacobean box-pews.

Dent became famous for its hand-knitting activity, which began in the seventeeth century and was still active early in the nineteenth. Robert Southey, in his miscellany *The Doctor*, which deals with the period of about 1760, referred to 'the terrible knitters e' Dent', the word 'terrible' meaning great.

Hand-knitting was not confined to Dent. The marketing centre was Kendal, a weekly wagon conveying spun wool to the Dalesfolk and collecting the stockings and other knitted goods. Knitting was an occupation for men, women and children, augmenting a meagre return from farming. Knitting songs enlivened the evening 'sittings in', when otherwise someone read aloud from the Bible or *Pilgrim's Progress*.

Dentdale's economic relapse began with the advent of the railway age. Tracks were laid at either side of – not through – the dale. The population today is less than half of what it was in 1904.

From the car park, cross the road, passing to the left of the memorial hall and to the right of the green. Where the tarmac ends, a rough upward track begins and climbs remorselessly through Flintergill (a gill is a small, water-carved valley), the beck being to the left. This gill, like others in the dale, contains an attractive mixture of indigenous trees, including thorn, oak, ash, rowan and hazel.

At a metal gate, look back for a view of Rise Hill, which has a neat grid-iron pattern of drystone walls constructed as Parliamentary enclosures in the mid-nineteeth century.

The large leaves of butterbur were used to wrap up butter.

The Flintergill track emerges from tree cover to enter curlew country. The long-billed birds may be seen in song glides, uttering a familiar bubbling call. Other streaky-brown birds of the moor are present. Skylarks sing as they rise almost vertically. Meadow pipits descend in 'shuttlecock' flight, wings and tail feathers held stiffly outwards. A snipe on the ground gives a 'chipper, chipper' sound, or dives in

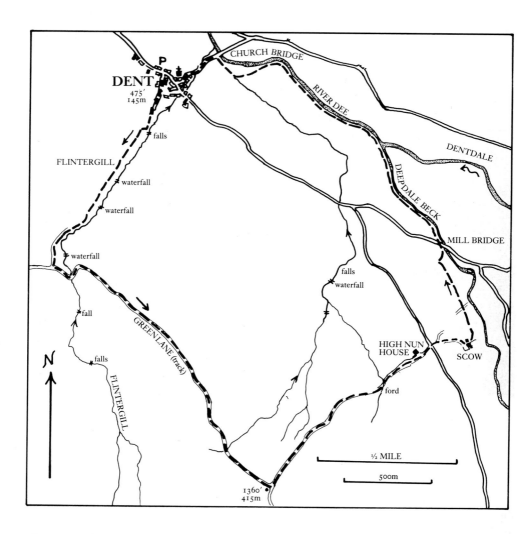

the air with a 'bleating' caused by air rushing through the stiffened outer feathers of the tail.

A wooden gate is negotiated; not far beyond, you will see a green road flanked by drystone walls that cost no more that three shillings a rood (seven yards in Yorkshire) to build early in the last century.

At a T-junction, turn left for an easy walk at high elevation along a thirty foot (9m) wide unmetalled road which, dating in its present form from the mid-nineteenth century, has climbed from Barbondale and is heading for Deepdale Head, where it joins the motor road. (Prior to the boundary revision of 1974, this area was the last flourish of Yorkshire, the counties of Yorkshire, Lancashire and Westmorland coming together at the County Stone on Great Coum.)

Dent Town, with the memorial to the locally-born scholar Adam Sedgwick (right).

Another T-junction is encountered and the road splits. Take the left hand track marked 'Nun House and Outrake', descending on a track of loose stones – still between drystone walls – on a route leading to Deepdale Foot. Deepdale, locally pronounced 'Dibdle', is a major tributary of Dentdale.

An iron gate is encountered. Beyond, the track runs between gnarled thorn trees, with a conifer plantation to the right. Two huge larch trees are seen just before High Nun House is reached. The stony lane is replaced for a short distance by smooth concrete.

The walker soon reaches the Deepdale road, which connects Dent Town with Ingleton via Kingsdale Head, the highest section having been made as recently as 1952. Look for a fingerpost marked 'Mill Bridge', which is half a mile away. Pass through a metal gate and follow a track to a wooden gate with a signpost indicating 'footpath'. To the left is a group of farm buildings. The route to be followed is now indicated by fingerposts and yellow blotches on stones. In spring, the banks are speckled with primroses and the many blackthorn trees are white with blossom.

A field limekiln, in good condition, is seen on the left of the footpath. Such a kiln is a relatively common feature of the limestone areas. It was used for burning lime, which had various uses, mainly agricultural. Arthur Raistrick, the Dales historian, evoked a splendid picture of a kiln with his description of 'a live spot of fire with the glow of the ash door flashing across the valley, or the column of drifting steam and smoke rising above the kiln and lit up momentarily as the filling settles within'.

When in due course the metalled road is reached, turn left, then right, a sign indicating a public footpath to 'Church Bridge'. A step stile leads to a well-beaten footpath around the edge of a field. A waterside path begins, firstly on the bank of Deepdale Beck, and subsequently by the Dee.

With a well-trodden appearance, the footpath becomes part of the Dales Way, a footpath of seventy-three miles (118 km) from Ilkley to Bowness-on-Windermere. Two of the small gates fitted to stiles (to thwart sheep and lambs) have pieces of redundant car tyre as hinges; elsewhere in the Dales, some hinges are made of welly soles!

The wild flowers are varied and prolific, including springtime favourites like wood anemone and aconite, survivors from the old woodland days. Butterbur, with its pink spikes, develops into a rhubarb-like growth which was once useful to farmer's wives needing cool wrapping material for butter intended for market. Perhaps its name is derived from this practice.

The path leads to the bridge near Dent. Walk into 'Town', thus completing the circuit.

WALK 2: TWISLETON SCARS, SCALES MOOR AND ELLERBECK

Start: Near St Leonard's Church, Chapel-le-Dale. Grid Ref: 738 772
Distance: 6 miles (11 km)
OS Map: Outdoor Leisure 2
Walking Time: 3½ hours

This circuit is at two distinct levels – along an unfenced minor road, then returning at higher level on part of the Craven Old Way, a former packhorse track between Ingleton and Dent. In good weather, the route offers views of the northern face of Ingleborough and a tract of limestone pavement. Also in view is the great ridge of Whernside. To reach the start of the walk, follow the B6255 from Ingleton for about 3½ miles (5½km), turning left at the junction indicating the church, just beyond a clump of trees. On Sundays, leave space near the building for worshippers.

The glacier which created the U-shape of Chapel-le-Dale cut deeply into the limestone. Notice, on the journey from Ingleton, how Twisleton Scars (to the north) matches up with Raven Scar (south). Glaciation exposed the older grits and slates on the valley floor. Rocks of these ages will be seen at close hand in the Ingleton Glens (*walk 5*).

Park the car in the vicinity of St Leonard's Church (or at some convenient place beside the B6255, beyond the Old Hill Inn). The church, built to serve 'Ingleton Fells', is now under the supervision of the Vicar of Ingleton.

A prominent memorial on an inner wall commemorates those who died during the construction of the Settle-Carlisle railway at the dalehead. The churchyard was enlarged and 200 people interred here. Notice the impressive gravestone of Job Hirst, a sub-contractor on 'Batty Green Viaduct' (now known as Ribblehead Viaduct) just to the right, within the lych gate. The gate frames a view of the dramatic northern side of Ingleborough.

Follow the unclassified road westwards to Beezley, the road crossing open ground for much of the way, so you may have grass rather than tarmac underfoot. To the right

are Twisleton Scars, extensive and majestic. Water seeps from the hill by way of a dozen or more becks. In wet weather, the disused quarry for roofing slate (in use well within living memory) has two spendid waterfalls.

The vicinity of Beezley Farm is reached after rather more than two miles (5km). On this walk, follow the footpath (right) which is signposted 'Scar End', this lying a quarter of a mile (½km) distant. Just beyond an old farmhouse called Twisleton Hall, a conspicuous path (right) leaves the major path and climbs Scar End with an easy gradient and a grassy surface.

Now your feet are on the Craven Old Way, used by foot travellers and packhorse trains heading to and from Dentdale. When it clears Scar End, table-topped Ingleborough is in view. The footpath has a fairly direct course of three and three-quarter miles (6km), remaining not far from the left hand wall, an impressive boundary marker which ultimately crosses the summit of Whernside, the highest peak in the Yorkshire Dales National Park.

The Craven Old Way is immensely old, judging by the fact that traffic has worn a route, a sort of causeway, through pavement and scar. The packhorses and

Around 200 people were interred in St Leonard's Churchyard, Chapel-le-Dale, during the building of the Settle-Carlisle Railway.

ponies sustained a form of transport developed in monastic times which endured in the Dales for some 500 years.

A packhorse 'train' consisted of from twenty to forty animals, with a driver and attendants. Many ponies were Jaegers (hunters imported from Germany). The fell pony bred on the northern hills was another dependable animal. Each pony had either a pair of panniers or a wooden saddle devised for holding the pack, containing such as wool, being bulky but relatively light.

Your eye will be taken by Ingleborough and White Scar, rising beyond Chapel-le-Dale. The footpath leaves the limestone for a tract of peaty ground, with an occasional light-grey boulder to remind you that this is essentially limestone country.

To the right are green, funnel-shaped depressions known as shakeholes or swallow holes. Also in view is one of the great natural glories of the district – the extensive limestone pavement area of Scales Moor, complete with erratics. These are dark rocks, alien to the immediate area, where they were dumped by the long-melted glacier. One extremely large piece of weathered limestone provides a focal point.

Scales Moor has great variety, ranging from an expanse of smooth limestone to areas where the pavement has been shattered into small pieces, the cracks

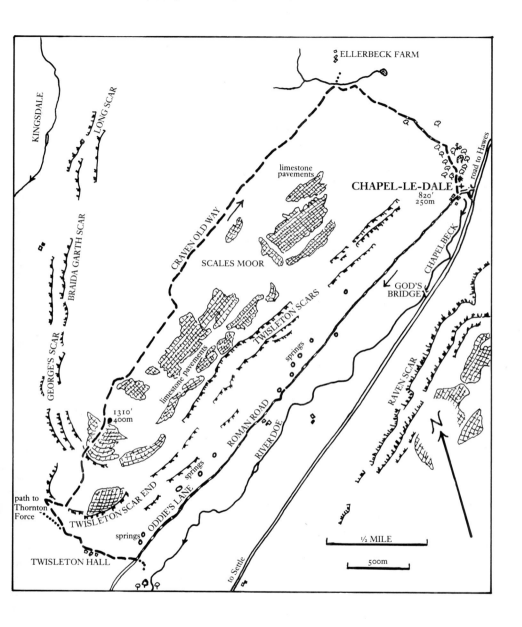

ELLERBECK FARM

KINGSDALE

LONG SCAR

BRAIDA GARTH SCAR

GEORGE'S SCAR

CRAVEN OLD WAY

limestone
pavements

SCALES MOOR

CHAPEL-LE-DALE
820'
250m

CHAPEL BECK

road to Hawes

TWISLETON SCARS

GOD'S
BRIDGE

springs

RAVEN SCAR

1310'
400m

limestone pavements

ROMAN ROAD

RIVER DOE

N

TWISLETON SCAR END

springs

path to
Thornton
Force

ODDIE'S LANE

springs

TWISLETON HALL

to Settle

½ MILE

500m

Dog's mercury is poisonous.

between them holding remnants of the old woodland flora, both plants and ferns, which have humidity and shelter from the biting wind. Anything that grows above the surface of the pavement is eaten by sheep.

Typical birds in this area are the moorland waders. Spring is slow to reach the high ground, but might be said to begin when the largest of those waders, the curlew, with its long down-curved bill, joins the local lapwings, which have a distinctive plumage of greenish-black and white, with a wispy headcrest.

Away to the east, dominating the head of the dale, are the piers and arches of the Ribblehead Viaduct, the most prominent feature of the Settle-Carlisle Railway, which uses the Ribble and Eden and the intermediate fell country, a total distance of seventy-two miles (116km).

The path to Ellerbeck becomes peaty, with adjacent bogs where sphagnum moss, the great peat-forming plant of the Pennines, is evident. The path is in line with a clump of trees which screen the farmhouse and main buildings, but these

34

are not on the route. On reaching a tarmac road, turn right to complete the circuit.

The last stretch is far from dull. Near Ghyllhead, where a seventeenth century farmhouse has been splendidly restored, the austerity of the landscape is offset by verge-belts of trees planted by the owners of Chapel-le-Dale Estate who, being conservation-minded, have also provided bird-nesting boxes. This area holds a large number of flowering daffodils in spring.

At the side of the road (right) is a piece of modern sculpture by one Charles I'anson, about whom little else is known. After standing here for years, the sculpture was taken in 1983 by mischievous folk and dumped in the lake at the bottom of Hurtle Pot, which lies just behind St Leonard's Church. The sculpture was subsequently recovered to be restored to its old position.

Green is the colour of trees and walls, for they are swaddled in mosses, an indication of the incessantly damp conditions and also the purity of the air. In spring, the ground flora includes dog's mercury and ramsons (wild garlic), which form a thick carpet, covering the litter of last year's growth.

Hurtle Pot (left), which may be peered into from the road but should not be explored, is said to be tenanted by a boggart, a supernatural creature of a mischievous temperament. A courting couple, startled by strange sounds coming from the deep hole, dashed away – to the amusement of an amateur violinist who had been practising down there!

WALK 3: WHERNSIDE FROM RIBBLEHEAD

Start: Ribblehead. Grid Ref: 765 793
Distance: 7½-8 miles (12-13 km)
OS Map: Outdoor Leisure 2
Walking Time: 4½ hours

Whernside's 'whaleback' lacks the sharp and dramatic outlines of Ingleborough and Penyghent. The route up the fellside from Ribblehead has been pounded into a peaty mush by many feet, but this peak is a 'must' for those who wish to stand at the highest point in the Three Peaks country. Have good footwear and waterproof clothing, and a map and compass are advised. Off-the-road parking is available at Ribblehead (B6255), approaching from Ingleton or (via the B6479) from Settle.

Whernside, an airy ridge eight miles (13km) in length, impresses by its sheer bulk and provides an impressive backdrop to a famous railway viaduct. A fingerpost near the small road bridge at Ribblehead directs the walker across the moor, which is called Batty Moss, heading towards the viaduct while remaining on the near side of the railway.

From 1870-75, this moorland held several railway shanty towns consisting of wooden huts, to accommodate some 2,000 navvies, mainly Englishmen, attracted from all parts of the land by pay which, at the start of the operation, was 10s (50p) a day. A typical hut had a living room, sleeping accommodation for the navvy tenant and his family, and a room set aside as a bedroom for any navvy lodgers.

The contractor's complex had a hospital, mission room, shops and hostelries, one being named the Welcome Home. A tramway, with steam-hauled trains composed of wagons, used by shoppers on Saturdays, connected Batty Green with other shanties, which had unusual names – Inkerman and Sebastopol (made familiar to the average person by the Crimean War), Jericho and Jerusalem (in the correct Biblical order) and, on the summit of Blea Moor, Tunnel Huts.

Where the viaduct now stands were the contractor's workshops and a brickworks supplying bricks for both the viaduct and the lining of Blea Moor Tunnel, which has a length of 2,629 yards (2.4 km) and is 500 feet (150m) below the moor at its deepest point. Local clay was used for the bricks, which were of such good quality that they were reported, when thrown from the kilns, to 'ring like pots'.

Salt Lake Cottages, near Ribblehead.

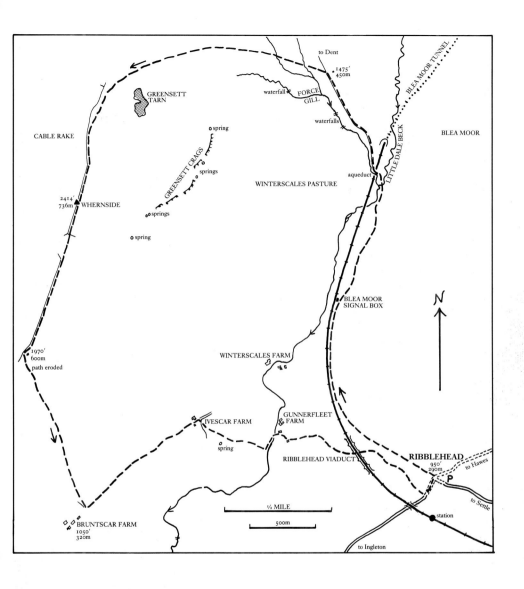

CABLE RAKE

GREENSETT
TARN

o spring

GREENSETT CRAGS

o springs

2414'
736m WHERNSIDE

oo springs

o spring

WINTERSCALES PASTURE

to Dent

1475'
45om

waterfall FORCE
GILL

waterfalls

aqueduct

BLEA MOOR TUNNEL

LITTLE DALE BECK

BLEA MOOR

1970'
600m
path eroded

WINTERSCALES FARM

BLEA MOOR
SIGNAL BOX

N

IVESCAR FARM

GUNNERFLEET
FARM

o
spring

RIBBLEHEAD VIADUCT

RIBBLEHEAD
950'
290m

P

to Hawes

BRUNTSCAR FARM
1050'
320m

½ MILE

500m

to Settle

station

to Ingleton

37

The twenty-four arched Ribblehead Viaduct.

The viaduct, with piers resting on concrete, overlaying bedrock, has twenty-four arches, a length of a quarter of a mile (400m) and a maximum height of 105 feet (32m).

The well-defined path to Whernside lies east of the railway, with a step stile on its way to the vicinity of Blea Moor signal box. The railway is crossed just south of Blea Moor Tunnel, where an aqueduct contains a lively beck. Notice, while looking northwards over Blea Moor, heaps of spoil from the tunnel; the rocks were raised to the moor top by steam power.

West of the railway, the well-defined track joins up with the Old Craven Way (*walk 2*), but almost immediately leaves it and, having the company of the Dales Way for a short time, passes within easy viewing range of a major waterfall in Force Gill.

The route to Whernside, used by thousands of Three Peak Walkers each year, crosses a stile, follows the side of a wire fence and then, with a turn left, heads in a wide arc to the ridge leading to the summit of the fell. Laid on the boggy ground are strips of durable material, to cut down the rate of erosion. Elsewhere, walkers' boots have pounded the ground into a porridge-like mush.

The Whernside tarns catch the rays of the sun. As the summit ridge is neared in spring or early summer, the whistling of golden plover will be heard, and you might see this attractive upland wader with the black and gold mantle and brownish underparts moving with mincing steps between the tussocks of coarse grass.

North Yorkshire and Cumbria each have a share in Whernside. A neat gap in the wall gives access to the trig point at 2,414 feet (736m). Ingleborough looms to the east and, far below, the Ribblehead Viaduct spans the low ground, the masonry being buttressed on either side by large embankments.

It is exciting to be on Whernside when a steam locomotive, hauling a special train, is throwing out lots of black smoke as it heads north. Trains are here on a rising gradient twenty-two miles (35½km) long, which became known to many a perspiring fireman in the old days as the 'Long Drag'.

The summit wall guides the walker to where a cairn marks the place of descent to Bruntscar. Confirmation is provided by wooden steps in the initial phase of the descent. Tread them carefully, for they have been damaged through erosion and use.

At Bruntscar, turn left for Ivescar, and by field path to a bridge over Winterscales Beck. Now pass under an arch of the newly-restored Ribblehead Viaduct to complete the circuit.

WALK 4: THORNS GILL AND DRUMLIN COUNTRY

Start: Ribblehead. Grid Ref 765 793
Distance: Over 9 miles (14½ km)
OS Map: Outdoor Leisure 2
Walking Time: 4½ hours

The head of Ribblesdale has one of the largest and most impressive drumlin fields in the land. This route begins with a small packhorse bridge, takes in an isolated farm called Nether Lodge, where several footpaths meet, and returns to the starting point on a more northerly course and with yet another single-span bridge. Park just off the road at Ribblehead.

A drumlin is a smooth hillock consisting of ground-up debris left in the final stage of glaciation. The map shows dozens of such hillocks, scattered around Ribblehead and to the east of the infant Ribble. When the sun is low in the sky, the shadow pattern draws attention to the undulations. The upper valley has a marshy character, the placename Horton meaning 'mucky farm'. In drumlin country you are bound to get your boots dirty.

Follow the B6255 eastwards. Several signposts will be seen; look for the one inscribed 'Nether Lodge'. The path crosses two fields to where Thorns Gill is spanned by a packhorse bridge which is like a rainbow arch set in stone. It springs, without parapets, from one rock wall of the gill to the other, having rowan trees for company. Until it has been restored, it will have to retain its rusting metal 'splints'.

No one knows precisely when this delightful little bridge was built. Local people used to call it the 'Roman bridge'. It formed an important link in a busy packhorse system long before the present metalled road through Selside came into being.

From the bridge, you will see a gorge composed of especially white limestone. The heady rush of Gayle Beck, soon to become the Ribble, has smoothed the rock. Notice the mini-potholes: within them are stones which, swirled by the beck, continue the process of erosion. It is tempting to explore the gill, but no right of way exists.

John Hutton, the eighteenth century clergyman-caver, walked this way and entered 'Catknot-hole', where he was entranced by the calcite formations. He noted:

'. . . the rocks jutted out, and were pendent in every grotesque and fantastic shape; most of them were covered over with a fine coating of spar, that looked like alabaster, while icicles of various shapes and colours were pendent from the roof . . .'

Over the bridge, continue up the slope, with views of a huge limestone boulder, shaped like a boot and holding a tuft of coarse vegetation, including heather, which grows out of reach of sheep. The path heads for the old farmstead of Thorns, now looking woebegone in its ruined state, but once a thriving farm and before that a grange (outlier) of Furness Abbey.

Furness, founded by Stephen, Earl of Mortain, in 1127, was endowed with lands at the head of Ribblesdale and Chapel-le-Dale. Though not good quality farmland, it

Gayle Beck flows through Thorns Gill. ➜

40

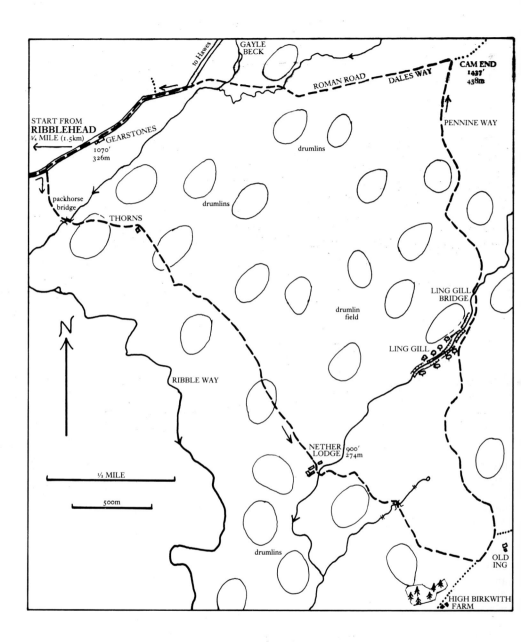

The purple flowers of wood cranesbill (left) contrast with the blue flowers of meadow cranesbill.

was valuable for grazing cattle in vaccaries (ranches). The placename Thorns was first recorded in 1190.

From Thorns, new fingerposts and gates help the passage via Crutchin Gill to Nether Lodge. In spring and early summer, the area resounds with the calling of the moor birds – the ringing 'cour-li' of the curlew, the reedy 'whoo-ip' of the lapwing and the musical piping of a redshank. Snipe dive with outer tail feathers extended, the wind strumming them to create a bleating sound.

Nether Lodge, yet another monastic grange in the 'wilderness' of the upper dale, is a collection of buildings of various ages, the farmhouse being comparatively

modern. The fields are less sparse and contain a greater range of wild flowers than do many Dales farms today.

Nether Lodge (first documented in 1537) is at the crossing point of many paths and bristles with footpath signs. Go through the farmyard, across a metal bridge, bear left to a wall stile, then right at God's Bridge (the limestone has been eroded to form a natural arch) and, continuing southwards, join the unmetalled road between High Birkwith and Old Ing.

The next stage of the walk is simple because it is also the route of the Pennine Way – by Calf Holes to the head of Ling Gill. Calf Holes is a name for an attractive pothole from which, presumably, a calf was

43

once rescued. (Each spring, the Cave Rescue Organisation usually recover a trapped lamb or two from this system.) Built into the single span bridge at the head of Ling Gill is an inscribed piece of gritstone, recording that it was repaired in 1765 'at the charge of the whole West Riding'.

In good weather, the moorland stretch of the walk, beyond the bridge, is a joyful experience. It begins on the old road up Ribblesdale. At Cam End, where you turn left on to the Dales Way, it has become a part of a turnpike which was once a Roman road, known to local people in olden days as the Devil's Highway.

The route descends to Gayle Beck, the larger of two tributaries feeding the Ribble. Gayle Beck has beds of shingle that attract nesting pairs of oystercatchers. An oystercatcher when sitting on its nest, a mere scrape in shingle, blends with the light tones about it. That same bird, when standing against the green of grass, looks a dandy, with pied body and long red bill. An exciteable series of 'kleeps' is uttered by the oystercatcher if anyone approaches its nesting area.

Beyond the beck, turn left and walk on the ample green verge of the unfenced road heading towards Ribblehead a short distance to Gearstones, the site of an inn which Lord Torrington, a visitor in the summer of 1792, described as 'the seat of misery, in a desert'. He unluckily arrived as the Scotch fair (a sale of Highland cattle driven on the hoof to be sold to the graziers of Craven) was being held on the nearby moor. The fair 'added to the horror of the curious scenery: the ground in front crowded by Scotch cattle and drovers; and the house cramm'd by the buyers and sellers, most of whom were in plaids, fillibegs, etc'.

Gearstones was converted into a shooting box by the Farrer family, whose Ingleborough Estate was based on Clapham. Victorian sportsmen arrived by train at Ribblehead, to be conveyed to Gearstones by horse and wagonette. A building across the road was demolished, but the nearby water trough, made of Helwith Bridge blue flag, remains. Was it to this trough that Mr Sharland, engineer of the Midland Railway, had a tunnel driven through snow one winter day in the late 1860s when he and his men, who were surveying the course of the new railway to Carlisle, were marooned by a blizzard? The old story is still told with relish in this district, as is the legend – for it is nothing more – that 'Ribblehead viaduct was built on wool'. The piers go down to bedrock and stand on a layer of solid concrete.

The circuit is completed by following the B6255 westward. There is open common on either side of the road, so you do not run the risk of being knocked down by speeding traffic.

WALK 5: THE GLENS AND WATERFALLS OF INGLETON

Start: Ingleton Community Centre. Grid Ref: 695 730
Distance: 5 miles (8 km)
OS Map: Outdoor Leisure 2
Walking Time: 2½-3½ hours

This route is a sortie in the 'basement' of the district, below the level of the Great Scar limestone, where the rocks are between 400 and 500 million years old. You will see mixed woodland, tumbling water, a ravine with its own viewing bridge and Thornton Force, where a river leaps from a lip of limestone and tumbles into a deep pool. Keep to the official paths and obey the commands on all the notices. Stout footwear is recommended. No charge is made for parking at the community centre, which is signposted. It is a ten minutes' walk from here to the start of the walk.

The Yorkshire Dales National Park publishes an inexpensive leaflet about the 'Ingleton Waterfalls Trail', its notes and diagrams explaining the local geology. This is of exceptional interest, 'faulting' giving the glens much scenic variety. Two deep and rocky glens accommodate the River Twiss (from Kingsdale) and the River Doe (from Chapel-le-Dale), the rivers blending their waters at Ingleton to form the Greta, which flows for five miles (8km) to join the Lune.

The Glens Walk was opened up by a Victorian 'improvement' society and was unveiled to the public on Good Friday the 11th April 1885. The Midland Railway ran excursions and Ingleton blossomed as a tourist centre. Muriel Humphries, who wrote up the history of the walk when the centenary was celebrated, foresaw the continuation of the Ingleton Scenery Company but added:

'One will never again see the profusion of wild ferns, lilies of the valley and wild orchids which once grew in the woods, for the people of Ingleton dug them up and sold them to the visitors.'

The walk begins at the abutments of a former railway, serving the local quarry.

Negotiate a swing gate and cross the South Craven Fault, a second gate being encountered at the start of Swilla Glen, an area between the South and North Craven Faults where beds of limestone dip at angles of up to fifteen degrees.

Swilla Glen, a delectable area, has an assortment of indigenous trees, mosses and ferns. Common birds are the chaffinch, our commonest finch, which is confiding whenever visitors stop to have some food. The chaffinch's loud call of 'chwink' is heard incessantly during the early part of the walk.

The titmice are present. These small, plump birds with very short beaks are familiar to all who have a bird table at home, and at Ingleton, in winter, they roam the woods in small mixed groups. The two syllable song of the great tit in spring sounds just like that of a rusty saw being used! The great, blue and coal tits often have a treecreeper for company. When feeding, this small and agile brown bird, lively as a mouse, works up the trunk of a tree, supporting itself with a stiffened tail as it pries into crannies for insects and grubs with its needle-like bill.

The green woodpecker, its ringing laugh more often heard than the bird is seen,

45

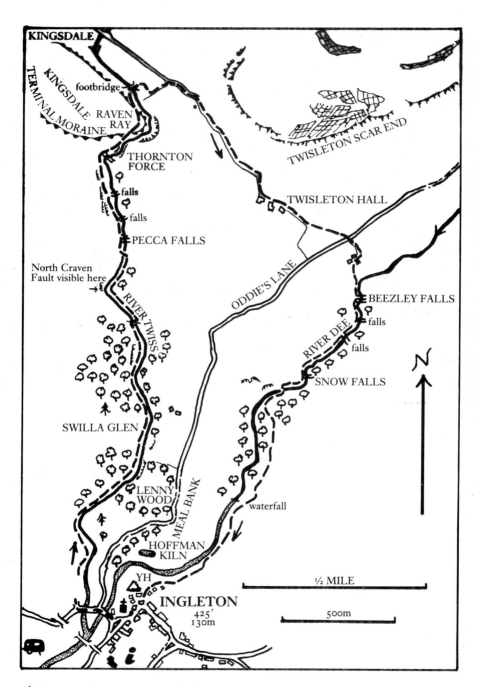

KINGSDALE

KINGSDALE

TERMINAL MORAINE

footbridge

RAVEN RAY

THORNTON FORCE

falls

falls

PECCA FALLS

North Craven Fault visible here

RIVER TWISS

SWILLA GLEN

LENNY WOOD

MEAL BANK

HOFFMAN KILN

YH

INGLETON

425'
130m

TWISLETON SCAR END

TWISLETON HALL

ODDIE'S LANE

BEEZLEY FALLS

falls

RIVER DEE

falls

SNOW FALLS

waterfall

N

½ MILE

500m

46

The green woodpecker's loud 'yaffle' call gives away its presence.

resembles a Dales parrot, with its green mantle, crimson crown and bright yellow lower back. A clear 'zit, zit' heard from the river is the call of the dipper, a plump dark bird with a conspicuous white 'bib'. The dipper is either seen perched on a stone or in arrow-like flight. The nest is a mossy structure, often near a waterfall.

At Manor Bridge, the walker crosses the South Craven Fault and enters an area where Ordovician shale is exposed. Notice, while looking upstream from the bridge,

that the left bank is composed of limestone, some of it adorned by yew trees, and the right bank is underlain by the much older blueish mudstone (Ordovician).

A few paces higher up, the North Craven Fault is evident on the opposite bank (a small cave is located on the line of the fault). Steps lead up to a stretch of path which offers a view of Pecca Falls. Five main falls are carved in bands of vertical 'grit' and 'slates' (known as Pecca Slates), which are of Lower Ordovician age (480

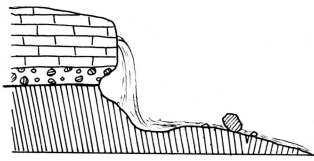

The horizontal Great Scar limestone is about 350 million years old, of Lower Carboniferous age.

The conglomerate at the base of the limestone contains boulders and pebbles of Ingleton slate, and represents an ancient beach deposit, when the Carboniferous sea invaded the land.

UNCONFORMITY →
(gap of 130 million years)

The almost vertical Ingleton green slates are about 480 million years old, of Upper Ordovician age.

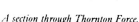

A section through Thornton Force.

million years). Water flows over green sandstone, which is interbedded with fine-grained slate. The different rates of erosion have produced the showy alternation of cascades and pools. In Pecca Quarry are displayed the ancient slates of the Ingletonian series, the age of which is not precisely known.

A refreshment hut stands in an area where visitors once fed red squirrels. This species is seen here no more; its American cousin, the grey squirrel, long esconced in England, has moved in. A roe deer, foxy red in the summer coat, with moustachial stripe and a kidney-shaped rump patch, is one of a species now seen in some local woods. If you hear a gruff cough it could be the alarm call of a testy roebuck.

The path, taking an almost level course high above the river, offers a view (left) of both the Ingletonian series and the Great Scar limestone. Into sight comes one of the major spectacles of the Three Peaks area – Thornton Force. To a geologist, it is something more than a waterfall, being also a

classic example of an unconformity, representing 130 million years of missing strata.

At Thornton Force, the water pours forty-five feet (14m) from a horizontal lip of Carboniferous limestone, below which is a bed of almost vertical Lower Ordovician slates. The tumbling water forms a bold, well-defined fall which has its force dissipated in a plunge pool. Boulders seen in the lowest limestone bed are what remain of beach sediments when this area was covered by sea over 340 million years ago.

A flight of steps leads up beside the Force. Nearby Raven Ray is a grassed-over bank, being the terminal moraine (the area reached by the glacier that occupied Kingsdale). The view from here takes in part of Kingsdale and the long ridge of Gragareth.

Kingsdale may be explored by following a path which turns off obliquely left from the path to Twisleton Hall. The Kingsdale route runs high for a while before descending to Braida Garth and on to the road up the dale. Yordas Cave, the mouth of which is set among trees, is on the left between here and Kingsdale Head Farm. Permission to visit this cave should be obtained from Braida Garth Farm.

The 'waterfalls walk' is well marked. Beyond a metal bridge, a field path leads to where there is a green sign directing visitors to Beezley Falls, beyond a road and farmstead. At Beezley, the River Doe roars through a ravine that is shaded by rowans. The dark pools contrast with Snow Falls, where the river goes white with fury. Take heed of the warning notices. The path consists almost entirely of concrete steps, leading along the edge of the ravine.

Baxenghyll, where the river is hemmed in by dark, sheer cliffs, has its own splendid viewing point (a metal bridge) at the end of a short cul de sac.

The walk ends in a former quarry, which is having its sharp lines moulded into something looking more natural by the slow weathering processes of wind, rain and frost.

Just visible from the path, but on private ground, is a low stone structure with several openings, all that remains of the Hoffman kiln, a German design once used for the continuous burning of limestone. A kiln three times as large, but on the same principle, was constructed at Craven Quarry, Langcliffe (*walk 13*), where the main part survives and, hopefully, will be renovated.

WALK 6: INGLEBOROUGH FROM CHAPEL-LE-DALE

Start: Near the Old Hill Inn, Chapel-le-Dale. Grid Ref: 742 776
Distance: 5 ½ or 6 miles (9 or 9 ½ km)
OS Map: Outdoor Leisure 2
Walking Time: Difficult to calculate, but no less than 3 hours

This walk takes in Southerscales, a nature reserve with a floral wealth best seen in late spring. The adjacent High Lot nature reserve, on the western side of Ingleborough, has a board walk which makes for quick progress through peaty terrain and tufty cotton-grass. At the summit of Ingleborough, you can either return to the car by the same route or, if two cars are available, and one has been left at Ingleton, the walk can include a descent by the popular Crina Bottom route to that village. The expedition demands moderate strength, agility, compass and map, and weatherproof clothes.

Ingleborough, at 2,373 feet (723m), is Yorkshire's most popular hill. So many admirers climb it that the major paths are well-defined. The most popular route is from Ingleton, crossing Storrs Common and passing Crina Bottom, a solitary building. After that, it is just a slog to the top.

You are recommended to climb Ingleborough from Chapel-le-Dale, crossing High Lot to a steep section of hillside which is in the process of being improved by positioning large stones to form an inconspicuous staircase. When the ridge has been topped, the summit plateau is a ten minute walk away.

If two cars are available, one might be left at Ingleton, taking the other to the start of the walk; both these paths may then be traversed, the second car being used to complete the circuit.

The walk, beginning at the upper level of the Great Scar limestone, takes in the higher strata – the Yoredale series. The actual summit of Ingleborough is composed of millstone grit, which is impervious to water and has thus allowed the mountain to keep its attractive shape.

Using the B6255 eastwards from Ingleton, park the car near the Old Hill Inn. The steep north side of Ingleborough appears to be blocking out half the sky. At the roadside, a short distance eastwards from the inn, is a small barn and near it a fingerpost, inscribed 'Ingleborough 2 ³/₈ miles'. An adjacent ladder stile gives access to pastureland with outcropping limestone. At the next stile, the Ingleborough sign indicates a course bearing left. Press on to a third stile, beyond which is a notice indicating entry to the Southerscales nature reserve, which is owned by the Royal Society for Nature Conservation and is leased to the Yorkshire Wildlife Trust.

(Great Douk Cave, a name appearing on some fingerposts, has a comfortingly large entrance and is well-lit from above by a natural shaft. The popular path beyond, leading up a wallside on to Ingleborough, is not an official right of way.)

Southerscales, which is part of the Ingleborough Site of Special Scientific Interest, exhibits features that are typical of limestone terrain – scars, potholes, pavements and grassland. An informative leaflet, complete with map, has been published. The path through the reserve is waymarked, by dabs of yellow paint on small posts.

On the limestone grassland is sheep's fescue and blue moor-grass, the latter having blueish-purple flower buds in

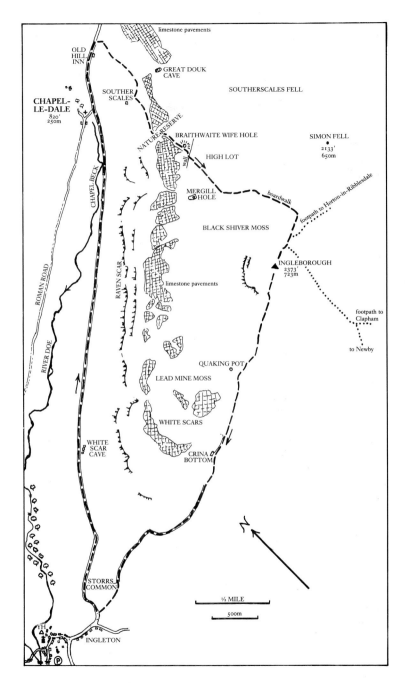

limestone pavements

OLD
HILL
INN

GREAT DOUK
CAVE

SOUTHERSCALES FELL

SOUTHER
SCALES

CHAPEL-
LE-DALE
820'
250m

NATURE RESERVE

BRAITHWAITE WIFE HOLE

SIMON FELL
2133'
650m

HIGH LOT

wall

MERGILL
HOLE

boardwalk

footpath to Horton-in-Ribblesdale

BLACK SHIVER MOSS

CHAPEL BECK

RAVEN SCAR

INGLEBOROUGH
2373'
723m

limestone pavements

footpath to
Clapham

ROMAN ROAD

to Newby

RIVER DOE

QUAKING POT

LEAD MINE MOSS

WHITE SCARS

WHITE
SCAR
CAVE

CRINA
BOTTOM

STORRS
COMMON

¼ MILE

500m

YH

INGLETON

The early purple orchid's leaves are often spotted.

Notice the white bib. A naturalist friend, visiting a ruined farmhouse, found a pair of blackbirds nesting downstairs and a pair of ring ouzels in residence upstairs.

From the sweet limestone area, the walker passes into acid grassland, edging on Braithwaite Wife Hole, which is said to be the largest shakehole in Yorkshire. This hole, caused when an underlying fissure absorbed the boulder clay, has a circumference of 500 feet (155m). Dragonfly nymphs live in the peaty pools.

The acid area holds heath rush and purple moor-grass, which have little if any value as food for farmstock. (The aromatic Yorkshire fog is another useless forage grass. A farmer friend used to remark: 'It grows on land that should grow better grass.') Other moorland plants on the skirts of Ingleborough are heather (mainly ling), bilberry and cross-leaved heath, which is unusual among the heathers in being able to thrive in waterlogged conditions, which it does by exuding oxygen to protect its roots.

The same applies to the cotton-grass, which is more common on higher ground, as you will see after climbing a ladder stile over a wall into the National Nature Reserve of High Lot. This (like the nature reserve) was once part of Southerscales Farm, being managed on traditional Dales lines which took into account the well-being of the landscape.

Progress across High Lot is rapid on flexible boarding, which was expensive to buy but quick to instal and has the prospect of a long life. Such boarding fits snugly into the undulations of the landscape and keeps the walker dry and clean in peaty terrain – which this is. From the board walk can be seen impressive views of the mountain's plunging slopes. In its early stages of growth, cotton-grass is the celebrated 'moss-crop', giving a useful 'bite' to wintering sheep. At its fruiting stage,

spring. Flowers include birdsfoot trefoil, fairy flax, wild thyme and, near the scar, the regal spikes of early purple orchid. At the side of the path, in the pavement area, are representatives of the extensive flora, much of which exists in the shelter of the grikes – maidenhair spleenwort, dog's mercury, herb robert and hart's tongue fern.

Among the bird species is the ring ouzel or 'mountain blackbird', usually seen at 1,000 feet (300m) or more above sea level.

The view from Ingleborough.

cotton-grass is unmistakeable with its cottony heads. (This 'cotton grass' is, in fact, a sedge.)

The ridge is attained by a steep but mercifully short climb on a path which has been consolidated and made easier for most of the way by large stones, forming a rough staircase. The reserve of High Lot is left by a swing gate.

The summit plateau of Ingleborough is close at hand. The Rev John Hutton, who ascended Ingleborough around 1780, summed up the experiences of the many who have climbed the hill since when he wrote:

'Though we had many a weary and slippery step, we thought ourselves amply repaid when we got to the top, with the amusement we received in viewing the several extensive and diversified prospects ... Of late years it has never been frequented by any except shepherds ... and the neighbouring country people, who resorted to the horse races, which were formerly annually held on its top.'

The formerly rich community of alpine plants has been destroyed by botanical visitors, who began to arrive as early as 1600. Light fingers still clutch at purple saxifrage which, to quote the Victorian historian Speight, 'may often be seen bursting into life and beauty while the snows of winter still linger about the hoary head of the mountain'.

If the weather is clear, walk round the plateau – which, incidentally, is divided

53

between the townships of Ingleton and Clapham – admiring the views. Southwards, limestone pavements crest Long Scar, Norber and Moughton.

Ingleborough is a supreme vantage point for seeing Pendle (south) and Lakeland (north-west), with a sparkle to the west indicating that the sun is shining on Morecambe Bay. The fifteen acre (6 ha) plateau is stony, with a sprawling cairn, a triangulation point and a cross-shaped windbreak incorporating a mountain indicator, provided by local men using a tractor and trailer for transport in coronation year (1953). When the present queen's grandmother celebrated her jubilee in 1887, a beacon was kindled on Ingleborough. The historian Speight recorded that the glare was seen from west of Leeds, some forty miles (65 km) away, and that 'upwards of 60 fires were visible from the tabular summit . . .'

Ingleborough was a focal point for Iron Age settlement, which was the period of the Brigantes. The massive hill fort, probably founded in the first century as an ultimate defence against the Romans, had the distinction of being the highest in the land.

A circular hospice, complete with battlements, was built on the eastern side of the plateau on the instructions of Hornby Roughsedge when, in 1830, he became Lord of the Manor of Ingleton. Unhappily, some of the stones were taken from the ancient structures. The hospice was partly destroyed by inebriated men on the day it was opened. Mr Roughsedge left the hill in disgust and, so it is said, never set foot on the summit again.

A compass is useful when it is time to leave, especially if Ingleborough has donned its bonnet of cloud. If it is proposed to descend to Ingleton, the route from the main plateau is the western path, by Hard Gill, Crina Bottom and Fell Lane. It descends swiftly to Ingleton, which is some three miles (5 km) away.

If the return is to be on foot, do not descend into the village but on reaching the B6255 walk towards Ribblehead for a short distance, bearing left along a footpath which connects Skirwith with Beezley, thence along the Roman road (*see walk 2*) leading to Chapel-le-Dale Church, which is not far short of where the car was parked.

WALK 7: HORTON-IN-RIBBLESDALE, THIEVES MOSS AND CRUMMACKDALE

Start: Horton-in-Ribblesdale. Grid Ref: 805 726
Distance: 7½ miles (12½ km)
OS Map: Outdoor Leisure 2
Walking Time: 4 hours

Here is a whiff of the wilderness – not too far from the car. This is the 'Big Country', with limestone outcrops and broad green pastures patterned by walls. The blue-black forms of Ingleborough and Penyghent form the backdrops. None of the terrain is difficult, but stout walking shoes and rainproof wear are recommended. Horton is on the B6479, which connects Settle (just off the A65) with Ribblehead. Horton has a (pay) car park and roadside parking is usually available between the Crown Inn and a by-road leading to the quarry.

Beside the gate at the approach to Horton railway station, a footpath sign indicates that Crummackdale is two miles (3 km) away. Ascend the short, sharp hill to reach the gate leading to the station and (after ensuring there is no rail traffic) cross the Settle-Carlisle line at the boarded section.

The station buildings are of a special type which became known as 'Derby Gothic', after the headquarters town of the Midland Railway Company, which began its regular Settle-Carlisle passenger service in 1876. The unused signal box was destroyed by a mysterious fire in 1991.

Horton's railway importance was largely bound up with traffic from the Beecroft limestone quarry (of which there is a good view from the footpath). It was developed in the 1870s by John Delaney, an enterprising Irishman who used the new railway to bring him coal and take away his limestone. In the old days, early morning and evening trains were run largely for the quarrymen.

The path through the fields is waymarked. Beecroft Quarry, with its turquoise pool (a consequence of deep quarrying for an outcrop of flagstone), was named after Beecroft Farm, which comes into view (left).

Having left the meadowland behind, follow a track between limestone outcrops. Beside the path are some distinctive plants. Whitlow grass, with its tiny white flowers, is named after its use for the treatment of whitlows. Salad burnet, a diminutive member of the rose family, with greyish leaves and green flowers, has, like many plants in free-draining ground, put down especially long roots.

Birdsfoot trefoil, its yellow flowers marked with red, sprawls on grassy sheep tracks and receives its nitrogen from bacteria in its roots. Traces of the old woodland days are found in areas where wood sorrel, with its delicate white blooms, is a common plant.

When the path shows signs of splitting, ignore the left-hand route and keep straight on for Sulber Nick. The path is indicated by the boot-worn rocks. A thorn tree (left) grows from a grike in a limestone pavement. The wall beyond includes up-tilted slabs taken from the pavement many years ago.

A gap in the wall has a waymark post (on the left). Cairns indicate the way ahead.

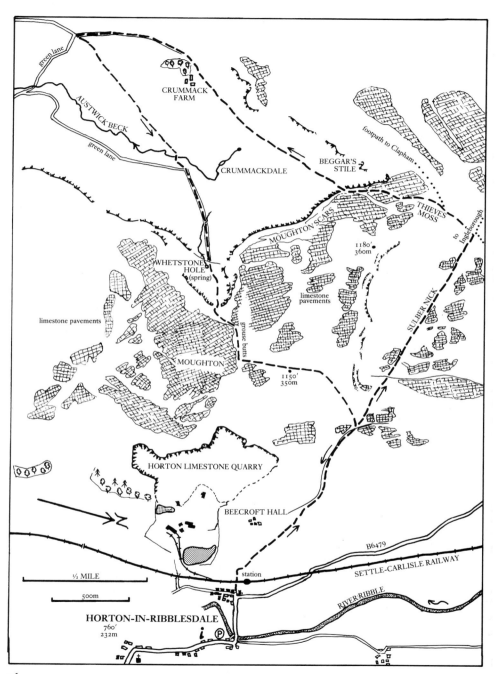

CRUMMACK FARM

green lane

AUSTWICK BECK

green lane

CRUMMACKDALE

BEGGAR'S STILE

footpath to Clapham

THIEVES MOSS

MOUGHTON SCARS

1180' 360m

WHETSTONE HOLE (spring)

limestone pavements

limestone pavements

SULBER NICK

to Ingleborough

grouse butts

MOUGHTON

1150' 350m

HORTON LIMESTONE QUARRY

BEECROFT HALL

B6479

SETTLE-CARLISLE RAILWAY

½ MILE

500m

station

RIVER RIBBLE

HORTON-IN-RIBBLESDALE
760'
232m

The path crosses a wall by a double stile. Among the limestone boulders on a grassy hillside grow lady's mantle, spear thistle, barren strawberry, lesser celandine, self-heal (probably brought up on the boots of visiting walkers), and (with one specimen at least clinging to a boulder) mouse-ear chickweed.

In spring the nesting lapwings wail as they circle. Notice the bird's head-crest and tufty wings. This species is known to Dales farmers as tewit, and 'tewit-grund' is a name given to marshy tracts of no special value agriculturally.

Having reached the highest point of the climb, the walker follows a path in a shallow valley called Sulber Nick. The Nick was created by faulting, there being a geological line of weakness. The walk is between attractive limestone outcrops, with a view ahead of flat-topped Ingleborough and its buttressing fells – Simon Fell and Park Fell.

The path, marked by cairns, passes through a peaty area where, this being boggy ground, lapwings nest. Skylarks, rising almost vertically like feathered helicopters, sing continuously. A meadow pipit in its stiff-winged song glide resembles a shuttlecock.

A fingerpost at a crossing point of tracks indicates 'Ingleborough 2¾, Selside 1¾, Horton-in-Ribblesdale 1½ and BW Clapham 3¾'. Turn left for Clapham on a path over springy turf. Beyond a wall stile, turn immediately left and lean on a gate to scan a remarkable tract of limestone pavement. In the distance is Moughton, with dark patches of juniper. Below lies Crummackdale. Twin walls stand beside the track leading down to the hamlet of Wharfe. This is classic limestone country, with bare ridges, scars, screes and mossy areas.

The imaginative can try to picture the passage of packhorse teams, which sustained trade and made deliveries between rural settlements up to the early part of the nineteenth century, when they became redundant with the spread of railways and other improved means of transport. In the packhorse days, the leading animal wore a bell to announce the team's presence, a device which was particularly important on narrow walled lanes.

At Sulber Gate, a dividing point of tracks, ignore the prominent track to the right of the wall (this is the way to Clapham) and instead go through the small gate on which you have been leaning, following a track downwards, across part of a limestone scree to where the path continues in grassy terrain. Bear right (the path goes south-wards), walking to the left of a prominent knob of limestone, which, in turn, is to the left of an area where some playful visitors have set pieces of limestone vertically in grikes, with a striking effect.

The path crosses a natural amphitheatre with the stirring name of Thieves Moss, leading to Beggars Stile. Recorded history does not tell us about the thieves or the beggars after whom Beggars Stile is named, though their stile has been replaced by a wooden structure over a wall and is not always easy to find.

To the right of the stile is a rowan tree, and in summer clusters of vermilion berries tempt birds like the ring ouzel, which are feeding up for their migratory flight to Africa. The rowan is rooted in a small crack on the limestone scar. Below Beggars Stile, where limestone cliffs form yet another amphitheatre with a carpet of lush grassland, are faint traces of walls and round huts which belonged to an Iron Age settlement site.

The path continues on a southerly course, keeping to the moderately high ground rather than descending towards Austwick Beck Head, which is not on the

Austwick Beck, Crummackdale.

official right of way. Head for the deciduous wood, the tops of the trees being visible. These trees provide Crummack Farm with *bield* (shelter).

Years ago, the shorthorn breed of cattle grazed in these large Crummack fields at an elevation of 1,000 feet (300m), the cattle yielding milk from which the cream was skimmed for butter-making. Crummack was renowned for its butter. The upland cattle are now of various breeds and crosses, being kept for beef production.

The footpath leads to a track, which eventually is flanked by walls. Just beyond where a gate spans the lane, count three telegraph poles (left) and then look for a lane leading off to the left. Turn into the lane and almost immediately turn left again

to cross a stile, near a fingerpost marked 'FP Horton-in-Ribblesdale 3'. This is the homeward stretch. The footpath is not difficult to follow.

Where the path climbs in an area of Silurian outcrops, common sounds during the nesting season are the chacks and whistles of wheatears. Both sexes have a conspicuous white rump. The male is a blue-grey black; the female being duller. These restless birds, forever flitting and calling, are at home in this little valley, where the bare bones of the landscape show through the green skin of the earth. Occasionally, the gruff voice of the raven is heard, and the large black bird with a wedge-shaped tail is seen in powerful flight towards Moughton.

The yellow-flowered tormentil.

After crossing Austwick Beck by a wooden footbridge, bear left to another stile. The head of Crummackdale is like a vast green bowl, with limestone scars on three sides and the summer pasture spangled with tormentil, a common plant in hill areas, and one which has a neat arrangement of four yellow petals and a protracted flowering season.

The next stile leads into the old lane connecting Wharfe with Horton. Turn left to walk on an up gradient (or what a Dales farmer calls 'upbank'). The lane climbs to a gate.

Moughton, with its flattish summit at 1,402 feet (427m), is worthy of a visit from, say, Austwick, on another day. On Moughton, the horizontal limestone, which forms immense pavements, lies over the near vertical slabs of the Silurian rock. In places, the meeting point is seen as an unconformity. Erratics (ice-borne boulders of an earlier age than the limestone on which they lie) litter the limestone.

The map shows 'Moughton Whetstone Hole', where a fine-grained mudstone outcrops near a spring. The whetstone was used for the sharpening of scythes and other farm implements. A piece of whetstone is often weathered and banded green and purple.

The footpath from Crummackdale to Horton leaves the valley where limestone scars are empurpled by wild thyme. At the top of the slope, Penyghent comes gloriously into view in the east. Walk a little further and look to the west, and the skyline is dominated by Ingleborough.

The path runs to the left of a line of old shooting butts, at the edge of an area where there is still much heather and the becking call of the red grouse is joined by the lonesome whistle of the golden plover. Head for a wall that is spanned by a wooden stile. On a fingerpost, the distance to Horton is given as 1¾ miles (3 km).

Follow a well-marked route to where you encounter the way leading back through the fields to Horton.

WALK 8: HORTON TO OLD ING AND BACK BY NEWHOUSES

Start: Horton-in-Ribblesdale. Grid Ref: 807 727
Distance: 7 miles (11 km)
OS Map: Outdoor Leisure 2
Walking Time: 3½ hours

This walk follows the course of the first good road in North Ribblesdale, one running east of the river and connecting with the Lancaster-Richmond turnpike on Dodd Fell. The return is on a footpath that traverses a limestone ledge, from which there are broad views of the upper dale. Wear good boots and have some waterproof clothing. Horton-in-Ribblesdale has a railway station, also a (pay) park for cars not far from the Crown Hotel, beside which the walk begins.

In 1812 the historian Whitaker considered that 'the beauties of Ribblesdale might be said to expire at Horton – and very abruptly, for at Stainforth a little below is all the verdure and cheerfulness of a Craven valley'. Modern walkers who enjoy semi-wilderness conditions will start their excursions at Horton.

Our starting point is the Crown Hotel (referred to in 1692 as the New Inn), or more precisely the lane which is reached by passing along the front of the building. Harber Scar Lane has an upward gradient for a mile (1½ km) or so. Initially rocky, lying between limestone walls, the lane has been well-trodden, for this was a monastic route used by emissaries from Fountains Abbey who had land at High Greenfield. The lane is on the Pennine Way and also the Ribble Way.

In view, across the dale, are Ingleborough and Whernside, with Penyghent (to the right of the track) showing up periodically. The route is on the demarcation between sweet pastures patterned by pearl-white walls (left) and rush-infested ground (right), where the grassy funnels of shakeholes indicate where water has found a crack in the underlying limestone and the clay above it has sunk.

Names on the map reflect the terrain – pot (hole), rigg (ridge), butts (used by

grouse-shooters) and mire (from the Norse *myrr*, meaning swamp). It was at Greenfield – in an area you will see shortly – that Arthur Young, the author of *A Six Months Tour in the North of England* (1771), reported one farmer's efforts to reclaim 'black moory land by draining, burning and liming it, sowing with turnips, then laying it down to grass with a mixture of rye grass, clover, hay seed'. The farmer improved and walled off over 200 acres (80 ha). Young was shown the benefits of the transformation – the land was carrying 20 horses, 40 cows and 1,200 sheep. In summer, 300 young stock were grazing the nearby moorland.

Summertime is when hatches of insects attract hungry rooks and jackdaws, dark-feathered members of the crow family, to the moors. Red grouse frequent the areas of ling and their voices are welcome in winter, when most other birds have left the area.

Curlews enliven the springtime with their song flights. This bird rises with swiftly-beaten wings; it hovers for a moment and then undertakes a shallow glide, filling the dale with a trill that begins slowly, quickens and ends with a few lanquid notes. This is also 'tewit land' (the nesting ground of lapwings), the birds frequenting areas where the ground is moist and insects and grubs are numerous during the nesting season.

A gate is encountered. The stile for walkers is to the right. Notice that some of the gate stoops in this area are of a grey, slate-like substance. This is Horton flag, which came from the laminated Silurian deposits at Helwith Bridge and was used for a variety of farm and domestic purposes – water cisterns, flooring and 'benks' (shelves) in farm kitchens.

Nearly two miles (3 km) from Horton, you arrive at Sell Gill Holes, the path lying between the holes. Potholers descend for 250 feet (76m) into a huge cavern, described by Albert Mitchell, a potholer of the 1930s, as being 'second in size to the Great Hall of Gaping Gill (on Ingleborough), roughly 150 feet high, 100 feet in width and 150 feet long. The floor of the chamber is a slanting bank of black mud, and the stream can be followed downwards until it disappears from sight between ... stalagmitic formations ...'

Beyond a gate, the footpath to Birkwith (1⅞ miles/3 km) goes off to the left. (This is the one to be used on the return from Old Ing.) For some, the walk to Sell Gill will have been enough; they should use the stile over the wall just to the left of the field barn and descend by a field path to New Houses, returning to Horton on a minor road.

Those who continue to follow the lane enter a vast and gently undulating countryside, with no signs of humanity beyond the futuristic pattern of drystone walls. In the dale (left) is a prominent sheet of water called the Tarn. Nearer the river, and not visible from here, is Tarn Dub, which receives water that tumbled into Alum Pot near Selside. That water flows *under* the Ribble and re-appears on the east bank, only then to flow into the river from the side opposite its source, a feat made possible by intervening glacial debris.

Whernside assumes the dominant

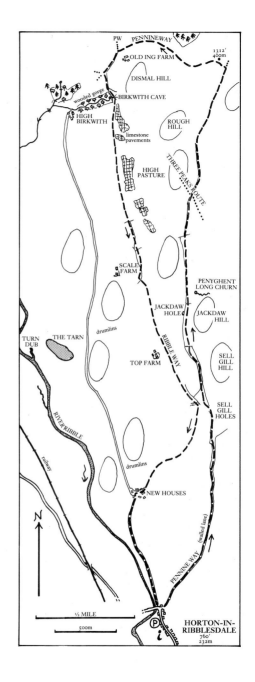

61

Harber Scar Lane (part of the Pennine Way) near Horton-in-Ribblesdale.

position on the skyline, with Park Fell (one of the Ingleborough group) to the left. Also across the dale, in a pavement area, is Colt Park, where ash woodland is established in the grikes, the trees sharing them with a large variety of plants. Colt Park is a nature reserve administered by English Nature.

A rickety iron gate crosses the Pennine Way. In an area which holds the gleam of limestone can be seen (left) a group of tall trees marking the position of Jackdaw Hole, a shaft known for many years, though it was not until 1936 that an inner series of passages were discovered and explored.

Rounded hills (ahead) are part of the impressive North Ribblesdale drumlin field. The terrain is covered with rushes (known to the Dales farmer as sieves). A hill to the right has a fringe of conifers,

marking the edge of Greenfield, a young forest planted for commercial reasons, though having conservational aspects such as leaving the best botanical areas clear of trees.

Two streams are crossed, and a field gate is opened (and closed!). The Pennine Way is shown by a fingerpost as turning left, and a boot-eroded path on a rough hillside heads for Old Ing, passing through a soggy area. Use as a marker a stone outbuilding, to the right of which is a stile giving access to more pastureland and, in due course, to a road composed of small and powdery limestone which would otherwise be wasted at the quarries.

Turn left for Old Ing, where there are two gates across the track. Part company with the Pennine Way, which goes off to the

A cock lapwing takes its turn at incubation.

right. During the descent towards High Birkwith, notice (left) a grey track which has a wooden sign with the wavy blue emblem of the Ribble Way. This is the path to take on the return to Horton.

At this point, some detailed instructions are helpful. Use the track for a short distance, leaving it where there is a wooded gorge (right). Keep fairly close to the wall, beyond which are the first of the trees, and thereby find a faintly marked track on turf which heads purposefully southwards. Within a short distance, another wooded gorge, protected by a wall, will be seen at a lower level; descend the hillside towards this wooded area. Just short of it, a stile will be found on a wall with, beyond the wall, a stretch of wooden boarding crossing a small beck.

Bear right beyond the little beck and proceed with the wall to the right (ignore the field gate). The views of the dale are enchanting. In due course, by keeping to slightly higher ground further away from the wall, the top posts of a field stile will appear to view.

This stile, to the right of a field gate, is the first of a number of stiles leading across pastures above Scale Farm and Top Farm, going on to a point just short of Sell Gill Holes where, it will be recalled, there is a field barn and the stile giving access to a field walk to Newhouses, a small settlement first mentioned in the fourteenth century.

The last short stretch to Horton is on tarmac. The circuit is completed as the Crown Hotel comes into view near the river bridge (notice that both stone and Horton flag has been used in its construction). The most prominent river bird is the stumpy, white-bibbed dipper which 'courtseys' while standing on a stone with water swirling around and, even when it is not in view, draws attention to itself by a metallic 'zit, zit, zit'.

64

WALK 9: CLAPHAM WOODS AND GAPING GILL

Start: Clapham National Park Centre. Grid Ref: 745 691
Distance: 5 ½ miles (9 km)
OS Map: Outdoor Leisure 2
Walking Time: 3 hours

The Ingleborough Estate Trail, for which a leaflet is available at the Clapham Information Centre, passes through Clapham Woods, goes beside the dark waters of Ingleborough Lake and returns to the village via Clapdale Farm. The walk described here uses the trail but extends it to and from Ingleborough Cave and Gaping Gill, a 340 feet (104 m) shaft leading into a chamber of cathedral size which can be visited (by bosun's chair) twice a year, when potholers organise 'meets'. Clapham stands just off the A65, between Settle and Ingleton.

Clapham, an Anglian settlement, evolved gradually and on a modest scale until, in the nineteenth century, the Farrer family (crest: a winged horseshoe) transformed the village, converting a farmhouse into a shooting lodge and eventually into Ingleborough Hall. The Farrers enhanced Clapham by restoring the church tower, greatly enlarging the body of the church and constructing to a new village plan many of the buildings seen today.

In about 1820, Clapdale was dammed to provide a head of water, used for domestic purposes and, fed to a turbine, to generate electricity for street lighting (among the first such lighting in Yorkshire) and to power machinery in the estate workshops.

Trees of many species were planted, and a carriageway made from the hall into Clapdale (previously known simply as Clapham Gill) and on to Ingleborough Cave.

Walk to the head of the village, on the side of the beck opposite that occupied by the church, and pay a small sum at Sawmill House for admission to the woods. The path zigzags gently up the side of an earthen dam to reach the edge of the lake, on which there is little birdlife, the water being deep and cold.

Limestone on the far side of the lake lies between the two Craven Faults. Reginald Farrer (1880-1920), writer, plant collector and one of the popularisers of rock gardening, seeded the cliffs with a variety of plants. It is said that in places he shot seeds into awkward places using a muzzle-loading gun.

Though born at the family house in London, Farrer was reared at Ingleborough Hall and, through the enthusiasm of his mother, developed an early love for gardening. This shy bachelor, with the hare-lip (over which he grew a bushy moustache) and a strange squeaky voice, travelled in the Alpine areas of Europe and the Far East, painting and plant-collecting, introducing into this country a great many plants, including twenty-four species of rhododendron, ten of which are still to be found in Clapham Woods.

Some of Clapham's specimen trees have iron nameplates near them. The woods have many surprises. In spring, a laburnum tree contributes a splash of yellow. In the steep-sided valley where the beck enters the lake (to the clanking of a ram water pump), Farrer cleverly exploited an exposure of Ordovician rocks in what is predominantly a limestone country by

The woodcock. Its distinctive 'roding' flight is seen at dusk.

planting rhododendrons, azaleas and Japanese maple. They are in full flower about May/June.

In open glades, in spring, are massed bluebells and snow-white patches of ransoms (garlic). Other common woodland species which thrive here are wood anemone, primrose, dog's mercury and wood sorrel. Woodruff is another white flower strongly represented in open woodland.

The woods are clamorous with bird song. Blackbirds nest widely and, at a time of clear-felling in the upper wood some years ago, nests were found on the ground. At dusk, you might see a woodcock 'roding', giving 'three grunts and a squeak' as it patrols its nesting territory, flying at tree-top height, with slow wingbeats, looking in the gloaming like a large brown moth.

The grey squirrel, a species introduced into England from North America, will almost certainly be seen, though until a few years ago these Clapham woods were the haunt of the dainty red squirrel, a native species.

The woodland ends for the walker with a metallic swing gate which squeaks when opened. The valley ahead is flanked by low scars and has a clear beck. Beside it is a small structure from which comes the rhythmic clanking of yet another ram pump – because it does not need an oil or petrol-driven motor, relying solely on pressure, it is an economic way of delivering water uphill to farms in limestone country. In this case, the water goes to Clapdale Farm, which you will pass on the return to Clapham.

·Not easily missed is a lofty cliff, at the base of which is a gash, marking the

An early cave explorer.

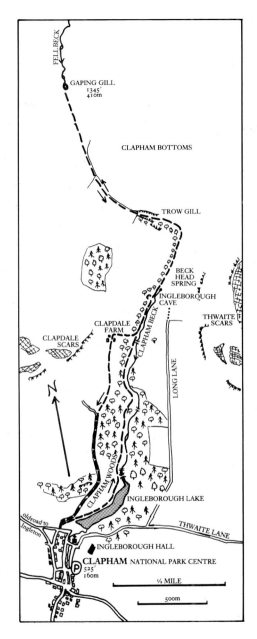

entrance to Ingleborough Cave, a system first explored in 1837 by the Farrers. They directed their workmen to break down a stalagmitic barrier at the end of the cave mouth – which became known as 'the old cave' – revealing long sections of 'new' cave decked with calcite formations, some of which were named – Sword of Damocles, Elephant's Legs, Bee Hive, etc. The cave is now ablaze with electrical lighting; earlier visitors were handed a three-pronged stick designed to hold candles.

Ingleborough Cave is 'open to view' for a fifty minute tour for which a charge is made. Little water flows through this series of galleries, the main beck from Gaping Gill, about one and a half miles (2 km) away, having found a lower level, resurging a little way up the valley at Beck Head. After many unsuccessful attempts, pot-holers wearing breathing equipment found a way through the complex system of linking passages in 1983.

The birds of Clapdale include the dipper and grey wagtail, two species which nest beside fast-flowing, pure water. The ubiquitous wren flits about the mossy stones and walls.

Beyond the cave, Clapdale is a narrow valley of grey scars, ancient trees and short turf. A cleft called Foxholes was used as a shelter by humans 4,000 years ago. The path swings to the left. Climb the stile to gain access to Trow Gill, carved out by the tumultuous rush of water at the end of the Ice Age and now a dry valley with limestone cliffs that are over eighty feet (25m) high.

The walker traverses a narrowing valley to a jumble of boulders at the exit point from the gill. The path runs to the right of a wall. Ignore the first stile on the left. In one area, the going is rocky. Features of this limestone country are swallow holes and several small open shafts.

Continue along the path to where a broad stile leads over the wall to the left. Thousands of pairs of boots on the feet of eager walkers have bared the stone on the final approaches to Gaping Gill, one of a number of large natural shafts in the Great Scar limestone, formed by streams which have collected on the impermeable Yoredale beds at higher levels. Fell Beck, which flows into Gaping Gill, rises high on Ingleborough.

The limestone lip of the main shaft of Gaping Gill is seen at the bottom of a funnel-shaped depression which has some wire fencing as a barrier. To go near the rim of Gaping Gill is foolhardy. The shaft leads into a chamber some 460 feet (140m) long, about 100 feet (30m) high amd 100 feet (30m) wide.

Gaping Gill was conquered by a Frenchman, Edward Alfred Martel, in 1895. Using rope and rope ladders, he began the descent in the early afternoon, when a

An impression of Gaping Gill at the time of Martel's descent in 1895.

storm was rumbling around the fells. The descent took twenty-three minutes. He explored the chamber and returned to the surface in twenty-eight minutes, to be applauded by a hundred spectators.

A modest man, Martel left a little note in the visitors book at the New Inn, Clapham: 'On Thursday, lst of August, I went down Gaper Gill hole, &c'. The first Englishman

68

to descend the shaft, Edward Calvert, achieved the feat in the following year.

Organised descents take place twice a year when pothole clubs assemble the specialist tackle needed – a gantry, winch and bosun's chair. The charge made for a descent covers the cost of maintaining the tackle. For many years the descent was free, but ten shillings (50p) was charged when the visitor was hauled back to the surface!

The path to the summit of Little Ingleborough, from which the main summit plateau of Ingleborough is attained, can be clearly seen.

Return to Ingleborough Cave by the route taken on the outward journey and continue down the little valley towards the woods. Before these are reached, a rocky path is seen extending diagonally upwards (to the right). It leads to Clapdale Farm.

According to a seventeenth century historian named Dodsworth, the house was fortified. He refers to Clapdale as being a 'great old castle joyning on Clapham'. A tradition relates that there is a 'secret passage' (a limestone cave?) linking the farmhouse with a point low down the hill.

From the building which once was 'Clapdale Castle . . . on the skirt of the high hill Ingleborrow' (Dodsworth again), there is a firm and steady descent by track back to Clapham, with views of the multi-tinted woodland.

WALK 10: CLAPHAM, NORBER AND AUSTWICK

Start: Clapham Information Centre. Grid Ref: 745 691
Distance: 5 miles (8 km)
OS Map: Outdoor Leisure 2
Walking Time: 2½ hours

A steepish climb from Clapham is followed by a stroll through fields and an easy scramble to the Norber erratics, rocks plucked from their ancient beds in Crummackdale by glacial ice and now standing on small limestone plinths. The starting point for the walk is Clapham National Park Centre, just off the A65 between Settle and Ingleton.

Clapham (once the settlement of a man called Clapa) was transformed when the Farrer family developed Ingleborough Estate in the nineteenth century. The grounds of their new hall were extended over Thwaite Lane, an ancient right of way, in about 1833. Tunnels were created, and these provide a novel start to this walk.

Turn right when leaving the car park. Walk along the lane to the right of the church and soon the sound of your boots will be reverberating in a tunnel. Thwaite Lane was a monastic route used by Fountains Abbey, which had widespread properties in Yorkshire and the Lake District. The section passing Clapham continues eastwards to the north of Austwick and on to a crossing of the Ribble at Helwith Bridge.

Thwaite Lane became a packhorse route. This traffic ceased in the nineteenth century. No longer was the distinctive clang of the packhorse bell, worn by the leading horse in a team, to be heard on Thwaite Lane. The historian Harry Speight wrote in 1897:

'When the packhorse traffic ceased, hundreds of these sonorous bells were sold for old metal, and the brokers' shops were for a time full of them.'

Beyond the tunnels, Thwaite Lane climbs steadily between mossy walls, protecting the estate woodland. Pheasants are bred and released for sport, but quite a number survive to breed in the wild. The crowing of this species is heard at any time of year, and as the birds prepare to go to roost in the trees.

In spring, the great spotted woodpecker raps its beak on a resonant piece of dead wood to announce its presence, and the 'yaffle' (shrill laughing call) of the green woodpecker may be heard. Of the two species, the green is larger and more likely to be seen, having a preference for open parkland areas. The great spotted has a dark back with white shoulder patches and, viewed at close range, a crimson patch under the tail-coverts.

At the junction, ignore Long Lane (signposted 'Selside 4¾ miles'), bearing right to continue along Thwaite Lane, which is an excellent vantage point for some shapely hills – Ingleborough (north-west), Norber (north-east), Moughton and Oxenber (easterly). The marshy ground between Thwaite Lane and Norber has the remains of an encircling wall which presumably kept stock out of the mire. It provides good nesting ground for upland waders. The redshank is distinctive, with its trim black and grey figure, bright red legs, and the white back and rump seen when the bird has taken excitedly into the air.

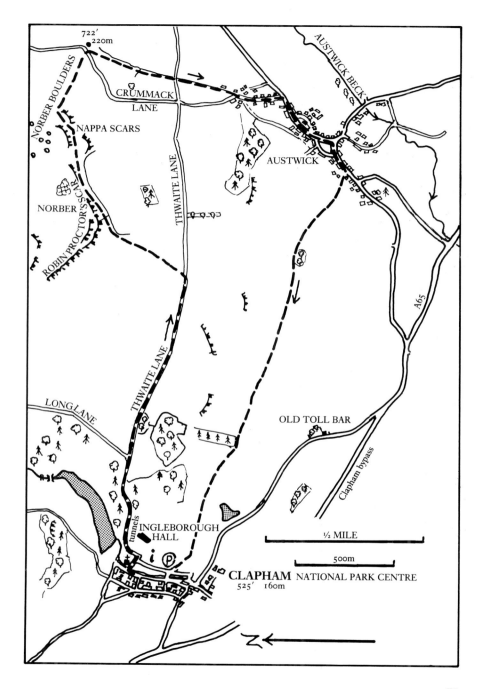

722'
220m

NORBER BOULDERS

CRUMMACK
LANE

NAPPA SCARS

AUSTWICK BECK

THWAITE LANE

AUSTWICK

NORBER

ROBIN PROCTOR'S SCAR

A65

LONG LANE

THWAITE LANE

OLD TOLL BAR

Clapham bypass

½ MILE

500m

tunnels

INGLEBOROUGH
HALL

P

i

CLAPHAM NATIONAL PARK CENTRE
525'   160m

Norber from Thwaite Lane.

At the second wall on the left, notice a cripple hole, which is just adequate for sheep to pass through but not cattle; it is a means of permitting mixed grazing, giving the sheep a wider area over which to roam than other stock. The use of such holes reduces the distances covered by farmers when driving sheep across country. The cripple hole beside Thwaite Lane is framed by pieces of Horton flagstone.

Just beyond this second wall is a fingerpost marked 'Norber ½'. Follow a footpath (half right) across grassland towards Norber ('north hill', in relation to Austwick). The main scar has long been known as Robin Procter's from some old-time fatality, the details of which have been forgotten.

The path runs near some limestone outcrops in an area littered with dark Silurian boulders, and climbs gently towards a signpost indicating 'Clapham' and 'Crummack'. Fork left at the signpost. (Mark well the position of the sign, to which a return is made after the boulders have been visited.)

The Norber Boulders, which now come into view, feature in geological textbooks throughout the world as a classic example of erratics, rock boulders which are not in their correct geological positions. These boulders were shifted to their present locations by a valley glacier which occupied nearby Crummackdale, smoothing and grinding the valley until it was below the Great Scar limestone and plucking at the

The wheatear may display its white rump as it flies away.

older, greyer Silurian and Ordovician rocks.

The Crummackdale glacier, its ice holding pieces of these older rocks, overswept Norber Brow. It was here, with the amelioration of the climate and the melting of glacial ice, that some large pieces of Silurian rock were deposited on an area of ice-scoured limestone. Subsequent erosion of the areas between the boulders left a few of the alien rocks standing on pedestals of limestone. One boulder has three limestone 'feet'.

In clear weather, enjoy the view of Moughton across Crummackdale, a dale said to be named by the Celts, meaning 'crooked hill'. Also in view are Pendle Hill and some of the Bowland Fells.

Now return to the signpost and step out in the 'Crummack' direction. On reaching a wall, follow it uphill to where there is a stile. The path passes by Nappa Scar. In the winter of 1990-1, a considerable rockfall littered the slope below the scar and the evidence remains there for all to see.

Keep close to the wall, crossing a stile to attain the Crummack road. Directly ahead is another stile leading into a large field, the path dipping right towards a beck spanned by a simple wooden bridge. Three more stiles and two gates lead the walker to Town Head at Austwick.

Here we are in Norse country, the name Austwick meaning 'a settlement to the east', presumably of Clapham. Norber gives Austwick some foul-weather protection; lots of the houses face south, over fields patterned by drystone walls, many of which were built during the enclosure of the commons in 1814.

It was at this time that a calf-bound minute book was started to record the 'herd-lettings', the appointment of shepherds for the 'stinted' pastures of Oxenber, Moughton and Long Scar. A stint represents the pastorage of a sheep in country so rocky that the term 'acre' has little significance. Each farm was allocated a number of stints, several of which might be used for the grazing of a larger animal, such as a cow or a horse.

Today, the farmers do the shepherding themselves, but still meet in February to discuss mutual problems like the stocking rate and repairing walls.

Austwick is a quiet, greystone village with several greens and an inn called the Gamecock. When the Claphams were at Austwick Hall in the last century, the floor of a room was sodded and gamecocks were set to fight each other indoors. There are also a number of seventeenth and eighteenth century buildings with attractive datestones above their main doors.

The footpath from Austwick to Clapham starts near Town End. Pass the church (left) and then cross the road to a stile leading into a field between a bungalow and a large detached house. The distance to Clapham is given as '2 miles'; at Clapham, a signpost is inscribed '1½ miles'.

Follow a field way, using wooden stiles erected near old stone stiles which had become worn. Most of the fields, ploughed and re-seeded, have the uniform green hue to be found in many parts of the Dales. This field way to Clapham is notable for the sight of lynchets (old ploughing terraces). The wheatear, named after the white patch on its rump, is seen where stones outcrop or walls provide perches.

Near Clapham, drystone walls give way to iron fencing, a relic of the Victorian estate of the Farrer family. Ingleborough Hall, their old home, is seen across the fields on the approaches to Clapham.

WALK 11: CRUMMACKDALE AND WHARFE

Start: Austwick. Grid Ref: 767 684
Distance: 4½ miles (7 km)
OS Map: Outdoor Leisure 2
Walking Time: Less than 2 hours

An undemanding walk, this circuit takes in the lower part of Crummackdale, offering splendid views, the opportunity to cross a simple clapper bridge over a lively beck and to walk down a walled bridleway to a secluded hamlet of Norse foundation which now is private except for the footpath. Austwick lies off the A65 near Clapham.

Austwick, a relatively quiet village, presides over its own Three Peaks – Moughton, Oxenber and Long Scar. These have stock-grazing regulated by an old system of 'stints' (units of pasturage) to conserve the herbage.

Austwick is handy to two attractive settlements of Norse origin: Wharfe (from *hvarf*, meaning a bend), a group of buildings standing against Moughton; and Feizor, pronounced 'Fazer' (relating to a *shieling*, where Norse folk grazed stock in summer). This walk leads through Wharfe and to within a short distance of hidden Feizor, which can be visited without much effort as an 'optional extra', though it is visited by walk 14.

Walk north-eastwards through Austwick, with the Gamecock Inn and the village school to the left. Take the first turn left, at Hobb's Gate, and follow the road up to Town Head, passing (right) a seventeenth century farmhouse with a datestone above the door and a traditional garden.

The large building of Austwick Hall on the left has a pele tower as its core, a pele being a stout tower used as a refuge against invaders. The hall is well screened by trees. Just beyond the dwelling called Victoria Lodge (right), turn half-right to a footpath sign ('Crummack') and wooden swing gate. A second swing gate is encountered (fingerpost marked 'Footpath'). Cross the

yard to a stile giving access to a field. Keep close in to the wall on the right.

Norber comes splendidly into view, as does Nappa Scar (with signs of a recent major rockslip). Look over the field wall (right) for a glimpse of Moughton Fell, where horizontally-bedded limestone lies

A wall made from upended Horton flagstones, on the slopes of Moughton Fell near Wharfe.

75

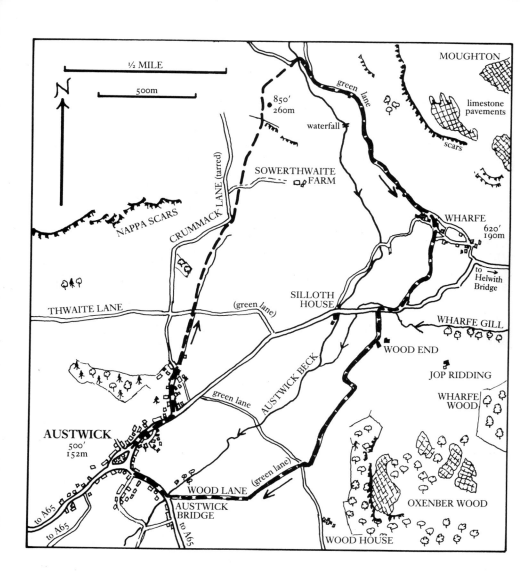

A clapper bridge in Crummackdale.

above the near-vertical Silurian rocks. The hamlet of Wharfe is seen lying in a web-like pattern of drystone walls. To the right of Wharfe stands Oxenber, unmistakeable because it is well-wooded, old regulations insisting that only dead timber should be removed. Trees grow from cracks in a limestone pavement which gives an unusual silvery sheen to the woodland.

Having studied the district from the vantage point above Austwick, continue the walk by crossing Thwaite Lane using stiles. In the sloping field beyond lies a footpath leading to a stile in the top wall. Go almost to the stile – then ignore it. By turning towards the right, you will see another stile, the first of a series leading to the bridleway descending to Wharfe.

Where the ground is boulder-strewn,

wheatears move restlessly, whistling and chacking. To the left of the path is a view of the whole range of Norber, its lower slopes having a coppery hue when the bracken fronds have died off. Bracken, an indicator of former woodland, fared less well when the many small-time farmers mowed it by scythe and transported it to their farms to be used as bedding for the young stock being wintered indoors.

Also from the path can be seen the solitary Crummack Farm in its half-moon shape of limestone scars. At this stage of the walk, the path descends to a stile, beyond which turn immediately left, through an old gateway, and then right for the clapper bridge, consisting of slabs of flagstone resting on uprights of unhewn rock. Now there is a languid descent by bridleway into the private hamlet of Wharfe, where you might walk but not drive a car, except for access.

Wharfe is entered near a fingerpost marked 'Bridleway'. Bear to the left, then almost immediately right for the exit lane, and at a metalled road turn right. Ignore the first signpost on the left ('Footpath to Wood Lane ¼') and look instead for the farm lane (left) marked 'B/W Wood Lane ¼ mile'. A millstone, let into the wall, now bears the name Wood End Farm.

As you walk up the farm track, look left to see the prominent V-shape of Wharfe Gill, carved by an ancient torrent of water from North Ribblesdale. The present beck is, in comparison, only a trickle. At the farmyard, bear right along Wood Lane, which ends at Austwick Bridge.

A point of local interest is the style of the gateposts, fashioned from slabs of Horton flag quarried at Helwith Bridge. The bed of Silurian rock being almost vertical and laminated, it could be removed in large pieces, some of which were transported to Silloth House, near Wharfe, to be prepared for use as brewers' vats. A few that were delivered to Tadcaster are still in use seventy years or so later.

During the last stage of the walk, a lane (left) may be used for a short detour to Feizor. Another lane (right) crosses Austwick Beck over the clapper bridge at Flascoe (a good picnic area, where the children can paddle in the beck) and continues to Austwick.

WALK 12: PENYGHENT FROM HELWITH BRIDGE

Start: Helwith Bridge. Grid Ref: 813 696
Distance: 9 miles (14½ km).
OS Map: Outdoor Leisure 2
Walking Time: 5 hours

A longish walk, this excursion includes an ascent to nearly 2,300 feet (700m). The green lane from Helwith Bridge is followed by a stiff climb over gritstone to the summit of Penyghent, descending by path and lane to Horton and returning by the Ribble Way. Helwith Bridge, on B649 between Settle and Horton, may be approached from the A65 at Cross Streets or Harden Bridge via Austwick. Wear good footwear and carry water- and windproof clothing.

Helwith Bridge is named from a river crossing. The present bridge spans the Ribble and also the Settle-Carlisle Railway. The old flagstone quarry, operated as such until just within living memory, was at its peak of activity in Victorian days. After a period during which rock was crushed into roadstones, the quarry was vacated, being flooded by water from springs. It is now stocked with fish for sporting purposes. Rainbow trout spawn in the shallower water.

The ground is private, but can be overlooked from the roadside. As a flagstone quarry, of modest size, it had facilities for 'sawing' the large pieces. The building in which this took place is the (now ruined) structure by the river. The 'saw' was indeed a piece of metal without teeth, the abrasion being produced by sand fed to it by water.

Start the walk, east of the river, where Long Lane extends from the B649 and a footpath sign is marked 'Dalehead'. Incidentally, widening of the B649 has left a stark roadside cliff which is a splendid exposure of the flagstone.

Long Lane, an eastern continuation of Thwaite Lane at Clapham and Austwick, now climbs between drystone walls by Dub Cote Scar Pasture to Dale Head and the road running 'back o' Penyghent' from Stainforth to Halton Gill. (One branch of the road continues by Henside to Malham Moor.) The lane is a vantage point for North Ribblesdale, Ingleborough and Whernside. Trains, toy-like in the distance, are seen clattering along the Settle-Carlisle line.

Modern techniques have greatly speeded up the quarrying process. Notice that Moughton Fell has been re-shaped and terraced. A good example of a geological unconformity, with limestone resting directly on the near vertical flags, is seen in the long-vacated Coombs Quarry, above and to the left of Foredale Cottages, which stand incongruously high on the side of Moughton.

To the right of the cottages are traces of the base of an incline railway, laden trucks from a limestone quarry on top of the hill providing the weight necessary to draw up the empty trucks for filling. Limestone quarrying at Horton has created a range of gleaming white cliffs, testifying to the depth and purity of the Great Scar limestone.

Long Lane loses its flanking walls and joins the Pennine Way on reaching the open fell. Follow the Pennine Way towards the 'nose' of Penyghent. The track is joined by the Three Peaks route coming up the hillside from Brackenbottom.

Half a mile (¾ km) of stiff climbing up the layers of rock forming the Yoredale

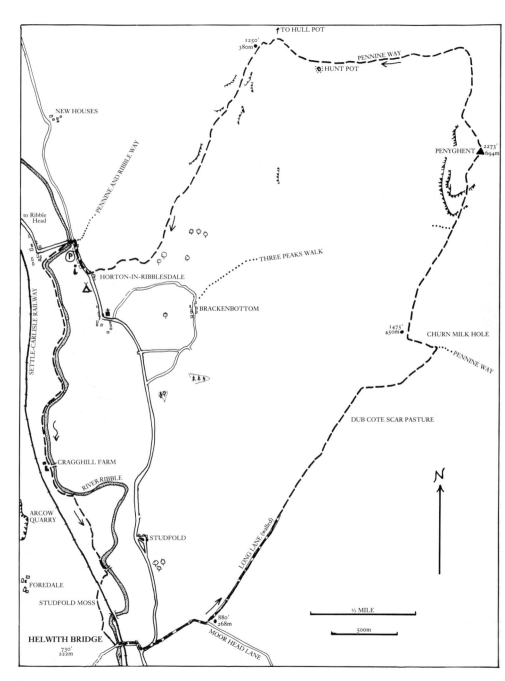

TO HULL POT

1250'
380m

PENNINE WAY

HUNT POT

NEW HOUSES

PENNYGHENT ▲ 2273'
694m

PENNINE AND RIBBLE WAY

to Ribble
Head

THREE PEAKS WALK

HORTON-IN-RIBBLESDALE

BRACKENBOTTOM

CHURN MILK HOLE

1475'
450m

PENNINE WAY

SETTLE-CARLISLE RAILWAY

DUB COTE SCAR PASTURE

N

CRAGGHILL FARM

RIVER RIBBLE

ARCOW
QUARRY

STUDFOLD

LONG LANE (walled)

FOREDALE

STUDFOLD MOSS

½ MILE

HELWITH BRIDGE

730'
222m

880'
268m

500m

MOOR HEAD LANE

The 'nose' of Penyghent.

series on Penyghent leads to its breezy summit at 2,273 feet (694m). It is the smallest of the Three Peaks. Looking eastwards, the tiny farmstead of Rainscar, beside the Stainforth-Halton Gill road, is dwarfed by the magnificence of neat meadows, tawny pastures and the long, lean Pennine ridges. Dominating the skyline is Fountains Fell, which takes its name from the abbey of that name in Skelldale near Ripon.

Ingleborough and Whernside claim the attention westwards, and in good light the lagoon which resulted from a section of Horton quarry filling with water has a turquoise hue.

On Penyghent (a Celtic name said to mean 'hill of the winds', though some people think it relates to a boundary), a deep croaking sound attracts the attention to a raven, a large black bird which seems to glide as much as flap its wings and is skilful in aerobatics. On the land around the hill are nesting skylarks and meadow pipits. The guttural calls of red grouse may drift up from moorland to the north and east. The curlew, large and streaky-brown, with its down-curved bill, rides the air currents as it utters its bubbling trill.

The descent from Penyghent to Horton begins with a stile over the summit wall and down a fellside which has degenerated

Helwith Bridge and Penyghent.

greatly from the pounding of thousands of walkers, runners and cyclists in recent years. The National Park authority scheme to remedy the worst of the erosion has resulted in a durable (if unsightly) path leading to Horton. The reinforced path begins at a signpost on the 1,900 foot (580m) contour. The impressive limestone pinnacle – a Pennine answer to Napes Needle in Lakeland – is nearby, but is not conspicuous from the path because it blends with the cliff behind.

A fingerpost marks the way to Horton, which initially is on that unsightly but necessary hard surface. In a shallow valley just off the Pennine Way lies Hull Pot, an immense, almost square hole which straddles a geological fault. At times of moderate rainfall, a stream pours over its northern lip. The pothole is littered with immense blocks of limestone which have fallen from the cliffs. There is no easy way of descending to the bottom; nor does anyone need to go there, as everything of interest can be seen from the top.

The Pennine Way goes southwards, along Horton Scar Lane, which is entered near a ruined shooting box. One and a half miles (2½ km) later, Horton-in-Ribblesdale is reached. Turn right. On the opposite side of the road is the popular Penyghent Cafe, car park and (through the park) a wooden footbridge leading over the beck.

Look for a footpath direction post and the wavy blue emblem of the Ribble Way (left) indicating the riverside, where the path runs through a wooded area before reaching the open countryside. Ribble Way signs provide a guide by the river all the way back to Helwith Bridge, where grey wagtail and dipper, sand martin and maybe even a kingfisher may be present.

The sand martin is brown in its colouring, with white beneath and a dark stripe across the chest. The eggs are laid at the end of deep burrows made in sandy riverbanks. There will be little time to concentrate on the kingfisher, most sightings being of a streak of bright blue as the bird moves low and fast over the water. If you do see the bird on a riverside branch, staring intently at the water, a moment's patience will be rewarded by the sight of its rapid dive for small-fish food.

A grey heron, standing like a wizened post by the water, or flying with its immense wings moving slowly, gives its call, a harsh 'frarnk', to advertise its presence.

The circuit is completed at Helwith Bridge, near which is a tract of old mossland called Swarthmoor, where pieces of flagstone, standing up like gravestones, mark the divisions where local families were once able to cut peat as fuel.

The area was also botanically important, with sundew and butterwort as two insectivorous, bog-loving plants. Much of Swarthmoor has now been spoiled by industrial activity.

WALK 13: STAINFORTH FORCE AND CATRIGG FORCE

Start: Langcliffe. Grid Ref: 823 650
Distance: 5 miles (8 km)
OS Map: Outdoor Leisure 2
Walking Time: 3 hours

This riverside walk begins near one of the few remaining Arkwright Mills and includes an eighteenth century packhorse-type bridge owned by the National Trust. The route takes in splendid waterfalls and a hilltop hamlet. Wear boots and take special care near Catrigg Foss. The starting point, Langcliffe, lies just off the B649, north of Settle.

Langcliffe (the village by the long cliff – limestone, of course) arrays itself around the edges of a large green. The church, an aisleless building opened in 1851, was built on the site of tanpits, where animal skins were transformed into leather. Langcliffe Hall, which has not changed its shape much in over 250 years, replaced a building that just qualified to be Elizabethan, the original datestone which survives being of 1602.

The Dawson family held the Langcliffe Estate for many years. A young man who changed his name to Dawson to inherit during a second phase of residence by that family was nationally known, being Geoffrey Dawson, editor of *The Times* earlier this century. It is related that when an elderly aunt lived there, she would not permit a telephone to be installed, so that when Geoffrey was staying here for a few days, and was needed by the London office, another telephone number was used and a runner sent to the hall to alert him.

At Langcliffe, inquire about the Naked Woman – a carving with a seventeenth century datestone on a building near the back gate of the hall. The building – formerly the Naked Woman Inn – replaced the house of the Swainson family, on which the 'woman' was first displayed, together with the date 1660. Incidentally, this 'woman' has a natty, well-trimmed beard!

Having reached the dale road, turn right and cross the Settle-Carlisle Railway by a new wooden footbridge which lies beside the stone bridge. A glance downwards reveals Langcliffe Cutting, with its wet rocks, scattering of trees and, in season, profusion of primroses, which happily are outside the plucking range of visitors.

Cross the road and descend to the Locks, where two rows of cottages were built for the workers at Langcliffe High Mill, situated at the far end of the mill dam. A cotton mill was opened in December 1783 by three Lancashire men, George and William Clayton and William's brother-in-law, who were friends of Sir Richard Arkwright, the famous inventor of a pioneering system of spinning by rollers so that a cotton thread strong enough to make a warp was produced. The Claytons had already established a mill at Keighley, believed to be the first cotton spinning mill in Yorkshire.

The mill is on private land, but from the road near the Locks can be seen the dam, with its varied birdlife. It is frequented by the kingfisher, mallard, moorhen and coot. The moorhen (a name derived from 'mere' hen) is a dark, chocolate-brown bird with a white streak on the flanks and white under tail-coverts. It is a nervous creature, moving jerkily. The larger coot is distinctive, having a slaty-black plumage with a

84

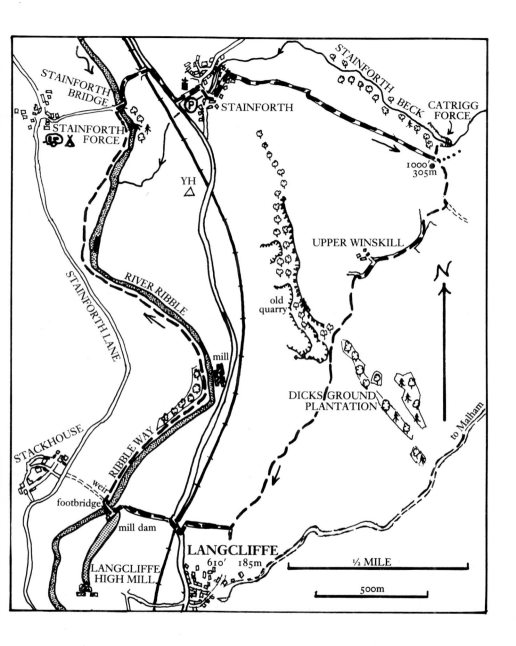

STAINFORTH BRIDGE

STAINFORTH FORCE

STAINFORTH

STAINFORTH BECK

CATRIGG FORCE

1000'
305m

YH

UPPER WINSKILL

RIVER RIBBLE

STAINFORTH LANE

old quarry

mill

DICKS GROUND PLANTATION

N

to Malham

STACKHOUSE

RIBBLE WAY

weir

footbridge

mill dam

LANGCLIFFE
610'   185m

½ MILE

LANGCLIFFE HIGH MILL

500m

Coot have bred on the former mill dam at Langcliffe.

white frontal shield (hence the saying 'bald as a coot') and white bill. The coot normally prefers a stretch of water larger than this mill dam, but the species has bred here.

Dippers frequent the dam but, more especially, the nearby river; these plump birds with the dark plumage and white 'bibs' are frequently seen perched on the stones or feeding near the weir at low water. A run of migratory salmon to the spawning grounds on gravel beds in the upper Ribble takes place usually in August, if there is a good flow of water. A salmon 'ladder' (a series of concrete-sided pools to assist the fish in overcoming the weir) now makes the passage easy.

Having crossed the footbridge to the west bank of the Ribble, turn right, a footpath sign indicating 'Stainforth Bridge

1½m'. Stiles are installed throughout. The river is never far away. Look for the red-breasted merganser, a rakish waterbird, smaller than a mallard, with a dark head and narrow red bill. The banks of the river are speckled in season with primroses, and a tract of woodland has dog's mercury, garlic and bluebells.

At the approach to Stainforth caravan park, ignore the field gate and keep to the right of the wall, crossing a ladder stile and arriving in the vicinity of Stainforth Force or Foss where, after negotiating several limestone steps, the river plunges into a dark pool. This is the place to visit when there is a run of salmon and a good flow of water.

The single span bridge, built by Samuel Watson of Knight Stainforth Hall in the

Stainforth Bridge dates from the 1670s.

1670s, has been owned by the National Trust since the 1930s. The composer Edward Elgar, one of whose great friends was Dr Charles William Buck of Giggleswick, visited the bridge in the 1880s and had a framed photograph of it among his treasures at his Malvern home. None of the composer's letters mentions the local ghosts – man and dog – said to wander between Dog Hill (near the railway) and Knight Stainforth Hall.

On the western bank, a little distance above the bridge, is a heap of stones, marking 'Robin Hood's Mill'. Robin was not the outlaw but a local miller who incurred the wrath of the Almighty by operating his mill on a Sunday; the mill

sank in a crack of the earth, though the mill wheels could still be heard rumbling. It was, of course, a natural sound in a local pothole. It has not been heard since it was investigated in the 1930s.

A by-road crosses Stainforth Bridge and the Settle-Carlisle Railway. William Riley, the Bradford author of many books, was inspired by Stainforth ('stony ford') and its 'singing' becks to write a book he called *A Village in Craven*, containing watercolour pictures of local characters by Elisabeth Brockbank.

To reach Goat Scar Lane, the rough track to Catrigg Force, either cross the stepping stones or use a path by the beck. You might be pardoned for stopping now

87

and again when ascending the rough track that is signposted 'unsuitable for motors'. The waterfall is a mile from the village, and the route to it is an unmetalled track with flanking walls. The views increase in scale and beauty until there is a glorious panorama, taking in Smearsett (the limestone knoll beyond Stainforth), Ingleborough, Penyghent and Fountains Fell, the latter's long, flat outline being distinctive.

Catrigg, a feature on Stainforth Beck, is a double waterfall largely hidden in summer by leaves, for the water plunges into a wooded gill. Continue the walk by returning to the lane and crossing the stile to the right of the gate to enter a large sloping field. Look 'upbank' and you will see the next stile in silhouette to the left of a field gate. A fingerpost indicates 'Winskill ½m'. Follow the direction indicated.

The wall to the right of the path has been provided with a splendid new cripple hole, for the passage of sheep. It is a larger opening than the average, with part of a concrete pipe on top and some flat stones laid neatly on the ground. A small wooden gate spans the entrance. So does an old idea take a modern form.

The walk continues along a well-worn path between walls which converge at a gate, with attendant stile. Cross the stile, and follow the vehicle track to the end of a metalled road connecting the hamlet of Winskill with the outer world. Use the gate marked 'Lower Winskill'.

Winskill was the home of Tom Twistleton, a Victorian poet. One of his collections of verse, published at Settle in 1867, is entitled *Splinters Struck Off Winskill Rock*. Tom was respected in his time and his examples of Craven dialect are cherished by some local people today. He was a modest chap and confessed:

'As lang sen near as I can tell,
I learnt to read, an' write, an' spell,
    But didn't learn mich grammar;
An', growing up baath rough an'
    strang,
I threw down t'books befoor 'twas lang
An' tuck up t'spade an' hammer.'

A signpost indicates footpaths to Stainforth and Langcliffe. Follow the Langcliffe path. The gate is at the start of a well-defined track between drystone walls. A fingerpost indicates the footpath to Langcliffe, and on the left of the track is the stile to be used. The next stile is near the far corner of the field.

Having crossed this stile, bear right and begin a gentle descent. The large pile of stones is significant, for it marks a path (to the right) leading down through a lightly wooded area to a small gate. The path continues downwards, passing the edge of the old Craven Quarry and eventually reaching a metal gate. It leads through a quiet area of drystone walls and emerald fields. The path contours to another gate, leading to the lane and, without further deviation, heads for Langcliffe.

Another footpath, connecting Langcliffe with Stainforth, keeps close company with the railway for most of the way. At Craven Quarry, it passes the Hoffman kiln, one of few remaining examples of a kiln devised in the last century for the continuous burning of lime.

The red-brick chimney was demolished. The long arched chambers, which were divided up into sections and through which the fire moved under controlled conditions, remain to help us recall a labour-intensive system. A team of men was needed to stack each section with blocks of lime for burning. Fine coal was fed through holes in to spaces left between the blocks. The Hoffman was last used for its original purpose in the 1930s.

WALK 14: GIGGLESWICK SCAR AND FEIZOR

Start: Giggleswick. Grid Ref: 813 640
Distance: 6½ miles (11 km)
OS Map: Outdoor Leisure 2
Walking Time: 3½ hours

Reference was made in walk 13 to visits to Giggleswick by the composer Edward Elgar. In the 1880s, he and Charles William Buck, a local medical practitioner, were drawn together by a love of music and outdoor life. Giggleswick Scar became, for Elgar, a Northern substitute for his beloved Malvern Hills. The present walk begins in Giggleswick, takes in the Scar and returns along a footpath offering splendid views of North Ribblesdale. Giggleswick lies just across the river from Settle and both communities are bypassed by the A65.

Elgar wrote to Dr Buck in 1888, shortly before setting off for another Dales holiday: 'Give my regards to Mrs. Buck. I shall be glad to get a whiff of pure mountain air again'. Giggleswick Scar water tops up the springs of Giggleswick and is also responsible for a steady flow in Tems Beck, sometimes known locally – to the confusion of visitors – as the River Tems.

The church, which has traces of Norman work but is mainly of the fifteenth century, is dedicated to St Alkelda, said to be a Saxon saint but possibly a Christianisation of a spirit attending a 'holy' well. Giggleswick School, founded as a chantry school, was presented with its royal charter in 1553. The conspicuous domed chapel on its gritstone knoll was completed in 1901.

The footpath on to the Scar now passes the rim of the limestone quarry (the footpath sign is on the southern side of the quarry entrance), but those who do not have a head for heights can walk up the Mains at Giggleswick, along an avenue of trees and, bearing left, reach a stile near a wood; a path goes diagonally right to the skyline.

Walkers on the quarry route pass the edge of a golf course, through which there is a path to the Ebbing and Flowing Well, first commented on over 300 years ago and believed to be caused by a double syphon in Giggleswick Scar. The footpath is marked and the well is at the side of the road near Buckhaw Brow. Be alert for speeding traffic.

At the lowest part of this area was Giggleswick Tarn, drained in 1837. An old dug-out boat was revealed and presented to Leeds Museum. Unhappily, it was damaged during an enemy raid on the city (1941), but has now been re-assembled and put back on display.

The path to the Scar is marked by a fingerpost inscribed 'Buck Haw Brow 1½'. The path climbs steeply, offering views not only of the countryside but also of the machinery in the quarry. Pass through a heavy iron gate, turn left and continue to climb on a path which meanders up the scarside. On attaining the top, it offers an outstanding view of Penyghent and Fountains Fell. A fingerpost indicates the line of the footpath (keep the wire fence between you and the quarry).

Yellow-topped posts indicate the route beyond the quarry; a spur path leads to Schoolboys' Tower, a Victorian creation which became the focal point for an annual race. The 'tower', a grand name for a simple rounded structure with a central depression, is now crumbling. As a

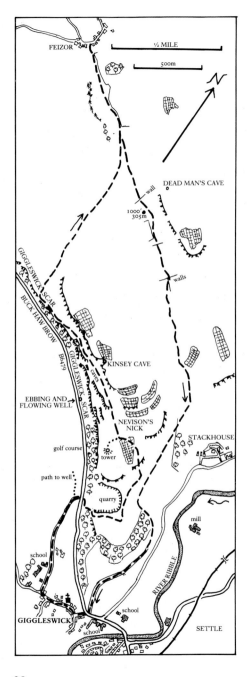

viewpoint it is outstanding. Giggleswick and the domed chapel on the knoll seem to be at your feet; beyond is the shallow Ribble Valley and Pendle Hill, looking like a ridge tent with one pole shorter than the other.

Regain the main footpath at a fingerpost. In the grikes of the limestone pavement are flowers of the old woodland flora. The early purple orchid stands out clearly against the limestone outcrops and sheep-cropped turf, flowering from April until the summer. The yellow mountain pansy has a patchy local distribution, thriving in areas where the leaching of the soil has begun.

As you stride along the grassy path traversing Giggleswick Scar, it is most likely that a kestrel will be in the area. The chestnut brown bird will be either perched on a tree draping the side of the Scar or hovering with slow-beating pointed wings while scanning the grasses for mammalian food.

The path offers a view to the left of Buckhaw Brow, a spectacular stretch of the old turnpike road which, until the coming of the bypass, was the busy A65. The trees on the left of the path are larches, part of the conifer wood on the side of Giggleswick Scar. A small valley on the right has a cave at its head.

Cross two stiles. Now bear to the right, ignoring the descent to the top of Buckhaw Brow. A fingerpost marked 'Giggleswick 1½' stands beside a wooden gate set in a wall. Go through the gate and follow the path upwards. Into view comes majestic Ingleborough. Having passed through another gate, follow the path that runs half-left and is visible for almost as far as you can see, passing eventually to the right of a walled enclosure, which is a small reservoir feeding a drinking trough. Keeping water on the surface in limestone country has taxed the wits of farmers. One solution was to make a dewpond, excavating a saucer-

The view from Giggleswick Scar.

like depression and lining it with impervious clay.

A sign marked 'Bridleway' indicates the path you have already covered but is a useful marker. The path now descends to Feizor. Notice a wooded hill (Oxenber) and moderately large village in the mid-distance (Austwick).

Feizor (formerly a *shieling*, where people took their livestock to graze in summer) was at a later time a halt on the monastic route from Fountains to their Lakeland estate. It has a 'back o' beyond' flavour which delights visitors. Stockdale House, with a water pump before it, was the home of the Clapham family, who also owned Austwick Hall.

Return to the gate by which Feizor was entered. The nearby fingerpost indicates 'Stackhouse 2 miles'. Walk up the hill, but ignore the bridleway sign, keeping straight on. As the hill is breasted, a stile comes into view, to the right of a field gate. The path is a deeply-rutted cart track. Beyond the stile is a large pasture with outcropping limestone. A wooden gate is used for access to the next pasture. Just beyond the second gate, turn right through another field gate which is not signposted. It is vital not to miss this change of direction.

Having gone through the gate, bear left along a well-defined track which becomes even more pronounced with the marks of wheeled vehicles. It leads through an area

A Victorian print of Giggleswick Church.

of limestone outcrops where wheatears 'chack'. Curlews float on the air as they utter their fluty calls. Young curlews, downy at birth and with short grey bills, snuggle against the ground and keep still when they hear their parents' warning cries.

The path reaches another field gate and makes a slow, winding descent to a gateway. The large field now entered has two stiles set in the far wall. The stile that you require is the one on the right. Cross that stile and then go half-right, entering a small beech wood, from which the 'yaffle' of the green

woodpecker may be heard in spring. A stile in the wall gives access to the path to be followed on the return to Giggleswick.

Stackhouse, which is shielded by trees lower down the slope, is a little-known hamlet, the roads within it being private. Here are found a few large houses, including a seventeenth century hall. The Dales writers Marie Hartley and Joan Ingilby have referred to this 'sheltered bosky hamlet where lilac and laburnum blossom in May'. Here, too, are majestic chestnut trees.

WALK 15: SETTLE TO VICTORIA CAVE

Start: Settle Market Place. Grid Ref: 820 636
Distance: 4 miles (6½ km)
OS Map: Outdoor Leisure 2
Walking Time: 2½ hours

The grandeur of limestone country – scar, scree and cave – are seen in a relatively small area just out of sight of Settle. This outing has the added interest of a 'bone cave', from which Victorian archaeologists removed evidence of human and animal life in the distant past. Durable footwear is recommended. Take special care on the scree below Victoria Cave. Settle was recently bypassed, lying just off the A65 between Skipton and Ingleton. Several (pay) car parks are available in the town.

Settle was granted its first market charter in 1248 and subsequently its several large inns catered for travellers on a busy cross-country route. The market flavour is still apparent on a Tuesday, when canvas-topped stalls appear overnight, like mushrooms, and large numbers of Dalesfolk arrive from villages and farms.

Settle's dramatic backdrop, a limestone knoll called Castleberg, may be climbed using an old path. The ascent is particularly attractive in autumn, for Castleberg – once quarried for its limestone – is now well-wooded. From a safe position by the flagpost, you see the market place, town hall (described as being Jacobean Gothic)

Settle's market dates from the thirteenth century.

93

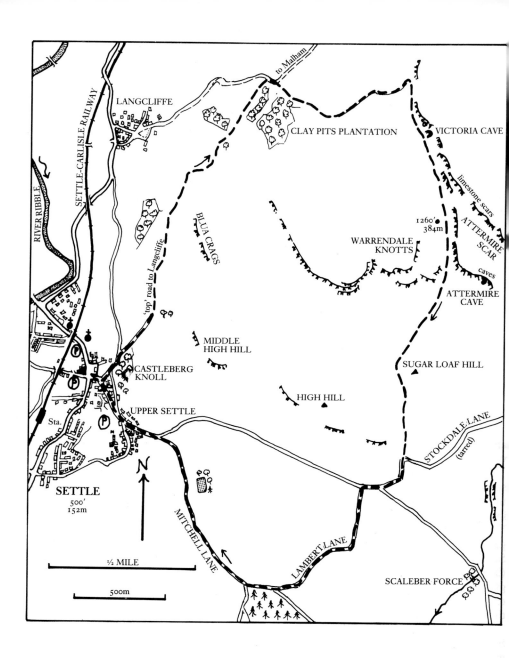

LANGCLIFFE

SETTLE-CARLISLE RAILWAY

to Malham

CLAY PITS PLANTATION

VICTORIA CAVE

RIVER RIBBLE

limestone scars

BLUA CRAGS

'top' road to Langcliffe

1260'
384m

ATTERMIRE SCAR

WARRENDALE
KNOTTS

caves

ATTERMIRE
CAVE

MIDDLE
HIGH HILL

SUGAR LOAF HILL

CASTLEBERG
KNOLL

HIGH HILL

UPPER SETTLE

Sta.

STOCKDALE LANE

(tarred)

SETTLE
500'
152m

N

MITCHELL LANE

LAMBERT LANE

½ MILE

500m

SCALEBER FORCE

The curlew is Europe's biggest wader.

and the impressive embankments and viaducts of the Settle-Carlisle Railway.

Upper Settle clusters round a green space; seventeenth century buildings flank the market place at lower level. Here is an inn – now a cafe – with the curious name of Ye Olde Naked Man, a skit on the extravagant clothing fashions of a past age. The Shambles is a prominent range of shops (below) and houses (above). The Folly, a grand building of seventeenth century date, can be seen within a few minutes' walk of the market place.

The South Craven Fault passes through Settle. Westwards, the outcropping rock is gritstone; to the north and east lies the pearl-white limestone. This walk is an introduction to limestone country. From

the market place, climb Constitution Hill (from near the Co-op), the road bearing left. Leave it almost immediately (right) to follow a rocky track which climbs steadily and at a moderate gradient to a gate, beyond which you will have grass underfoot.

Settle is now seen in the context of hill and dale. Notice, beyond the gaping hole of a quarry on Giggleswick Scar, the flat-topped form of Ingleborough. Walk with the wall to the left, ignoring the sign for Malham. Pass through a gate into an area where two drystone walls are close together. A glance into the valley reveals the eighteenth century Langcliffe High Mill (*walk 13*).

A gentle slope is negotiated, and when

the skyline is broken there is a splendid clear-weather view of Penyghent. The path lies close to the wall (left). A stile of darkish hue should be ignored in favour of following the wall to another stile.

The hillside, part of the Langcliffe Estate, has several small woods, composed of mature beech trees and ring-walled to keep out sheep, resulting in a rich undercover of plants. The local birdlife includes the green woodpecker, recognised by its laughing cry.

The path makes upward progress, half-right, towards a gate set in a wall, just below a wood. Go through the gate, then contour, using other gates, passing other tracts of woodland, to where the footpath joins a road which is completing its winding ascent up the brow from Langcliffe to Malham Moor.

Having joined the road, leave it within a short distance to follow a track (right) alongside woodland to a cattle grid. The pastureland includes typical damp terrain where the lapwing or green plover, the dark bird with a headcrest, lays its pear-shaped eggs in a slight depression on the ground. This species is somewhat colonial, with up to twenty pairs in a suitable damp area. The pied wagtail, a slender black and white bird with a long tail, is fond of nesting in crannies in the drystone walls.

Curlews make the area ring with their calls. Birds that have wintered on low ground or near the coast return to the breeding grounds in mid-March, though they will flock again if there is a drastic change in the weather with the onset of snow.

Ahead is a range of limestone scars which look especially bright against a summer sky. Immediately beyond a metal gate, take a sharp right turn to a stile with an attendant fingerpost inscribed 'Stockdale Lane (1½ miles)'. Climb over the stile. A path runs beside a wall, with the screes and

cliffs of Langcliffe Scar to the left.

The footpath becomes rocky and progress is correspondingly slower. Cross another stile, set in a short wooden fence. Jackdaws, which nest in cracks and crannies on the scars, are heard uttering metallic calls. Where the scree gives way to grassland, look for a path of beaten earth that climbs left.

This path takes a moderately steep course, partly on scree, passing the mouth of a cave (left) to eventually attain Victoria Cave. The vast mouth of this cave appears to view with dramatic suddenness as you reach the top of the slope.

Victoria Cave is a yawning hole, having been excavated by nineteenth century archaeologists. What turned out to be a repository of animal and human remains deposited over a period of about 120,000 years was rediscovered in May 1838 by Michael Horner and friends, who were out with terriers in an area known as the Fox Holes. At that time the base of the scar was a mass of sediment. One of the dogs entered a 'foxhole' and reappeared shortly afterwards from one at a higher level. Stones were pulled away and Michael crawled underground, the first man to enter for over 1,000 years.

Michael's employer, a Settle plumber called Joseph Jackson, devoted much spare time to exploring the cave, and he made splendid finds of objects left by early man. In 1869, a Settle cave committee was formed which received support from the British Association.

Briefly, in Victoria Cave were two layers of cave earth, with a thick deposit of clay between them. In the lower cave earth, and associated with the warm part of an interglacial period, were the remains of woolly hippopotamus, straight-tusked elephant and slender-nosed rhinoceros. It is theorised that, at this time, Victoria Cave was a den for hyena.

A caveman in limestone country.

The thick layer of clay was associated with glaciation; thus, anything found above it had been deposited since the end of the Ice Age. The upper cave earth held the remains of a fauna adapted to extreme cold, such as reindeer and Arctic fox, and also the remains of Mesolithic hunters, with traces, laid down many years later, of an Iron Age settlement some 2,000 years old. The presence of a number of valuable objects such as rings, coins, armlets and dragonesque brooches leads one to think it was at some time a place of burial.

Victoria Cave is easily explored. Virtually all there is can be seen at a glance. On the ground are boulders and mud, some dry and other areas greasy. The few passages are short and dirty. A cold snap in winter transforms the cave by decorating it with large icicles.

Return (with great care) to the path at the wallside and follow it to a stile, beyond which the path on open ground is self-evident, having been well used. It reaches the head of a rock-strewn slope, by which the walker descends with a view of a large tract of marshy ground called Attermire, said to have been named at a time when it was a lake with otters.

The valley is Stockdale and the beck is on the line of a geological fault, with gritstone to the east. Stockdale is the haunt of curlew and lapwing, redshank, snipe and wheatear, the latter nesting in burrows on rocky hillsides.

Descend the slope and turn right through a gateway which has but one complete gate stoop, the other being just a stump. You will pass several large pieces of metal which have targets marked on them. These are the remains of a shooting range used by local volunteer soldiers over the past 100 years or so.

Ignore a signpost indicating 'Settle 1½ miles' unless you are feeling tired and wish to use the shortest way back to town, via the Banks. Instead, cross the stile for 'Highside Lane', passing to the west of Sugar Loaf Hill. The views are extensive; looking back you will see the limestone, with its rock turrets and gleaming scars. The footpath leads to the road into Stockdale.

Having crossed a stile and turned right for the Settle-Kirkby Malham road, go right again for a short distance and then turn left into Mitchell Lane, an attractive green track between high gritstone walls and beside barns. It leads to the edge of a conifered tract and a metalled road at the top of a hill descending to upper Settle.

At the metalled road you are at the Settle end of the old moorland road from Long Preston which, in pre-turnpike days, crossed Hunter Park and descended into Upper Settle. Local people used to call it the Judges Road, as it was part of the King's Justices 'riding circuit' from one assize town to another.

The views include Whelpstone Crag, Giggleswick Scar, Ingleborough and – taken in at one glance – the old town of Settle.

WALK 16: MALHAM TARN, MIDDLE HOUSE AND THE MONKS' ROAD

Start: Parking ground just off the unclassified road near the outflow from Malham
                Tarn. Grid Ref: 894 658
Distance: 3¾ miles (6 km)
OS Map: Outdoor Leisure 10
Walking Time: 2 hours

Malham Tarn is the central feature of a township of rather more than 11,000 acres, the highest point of the moor being Fountains Fell. The tarn, on its bed of slate, is a famous study area for geographers and botanists, courses being held at the mini-mansion on the northern side which has been a field centre for over forty years. Travel to the parking area near the outflow of Malham Tarn from the village of Malham or from Langcliffe.

Early peoples found tolerable living conditions on these free-draining limestone uplands when the valleys were swampy. Norse folk kept sheep on the moor.

In the twelfth century, the people's distinctive pastoral way of life was incorporated in the estate of Fountains Abbey, who had been given the land by pious families. Water Houses, a settlement near the tarn, was first mentioned in the *Memorandum Book* of the abbey in 1454, when a reference was paid to a pig sold to William Tollar 'de Malwaterhous'.

The tarn, a stretch of open water covering 153 acres (62 ha), exists in a limestone country because its bed is formed of more ancient impervious rock. Behind Malham Tarn House is woodland planted by former owners, the Listers and Morrisons. About 1780, the Listers raised the level of the tarn by damming at the outflow, so the tarn's water level is artificially high.

Bird activity is curtailed during a winter 'freeze-up', though conditions are rarely as severe as they were in 1881, when one of Walter Morrison's estate men rode across the frozen tarn on his horse. Woodmen transported timber by the same route, using a sledge.

Breeding birds include the teal, the smallest of the European ducks. The drake, when seen some way off (as is usually the case), is distinguishable by its dark head and grey body. A tufted duck is a dandy, the drake having a black and white plumage. This species has bred at Malham Tarn since early in this century. Coot are relatively common.

The great crested grebe, here at one of its highest breeding areas, is large but floats low in the water; the tail is not visible. In the nesting season, this grebe has dark ear-tufts and chestnut and black frills on the sides of its head. Nesting is restricted by a shortage of suitable reedy areas where the floating nest, a soggy mass, may be constructed.

Of the mammals, the roe deer is periodically seen in the woods, and the plantlife has been studied as intensely as any other area of the country. Flowers are profuse in this area, where conditions include outcropping limestone and bogland.

Among the limestone plants, none is more attractive than the birdseye primrose, with its pink flowers and yellow 'throats'

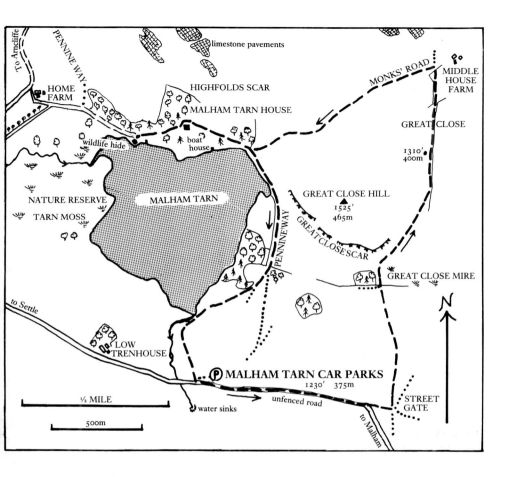

rising from a mealy rosette of leaves, a feature which gives it an alternative name, mealy primrose. It may be found growing beside the approach road to Malham Tarn House.

Having parked the car as recommended, resist the temptation to hasten to the edge of the tarn. Follow the unfenced road (eastwards) to Street Gate, turning left to walk along the hard track – a bridleway – which leads to Middle House Farm, pos-

sibly the highest situated and inhabited farmstead in the county. Its name relates to its position between Malham and Arncliffe.

Near Great Close Mire is a cattle grid with an attendant fingerpost inscribed 'Arncliffe via Middle House 4'. The track passes to the right of Great Close Hill, an area of around 600 acres (240 ha) where, in the eighteenth century, some famous sales of Scottish cattle took place, the customers being the graziers of Craven.

*The birdseye primrose is found only in Yorkshire,
Durham and Cumbria.*

According to Thomas Hurtley, the
Malham schoolmaster – who was not a very
reliable historian – a Skipton grazier, Mr
Birtwhistle, rented land on Great Close for
the sale of cattle he bought on trips to
wildest Caledonia. This grazier was supposed to have had 'Twenty Thousand head
of Cattle on this field in one summer, every
Herd enticed from their native soil and
ushered into this fragrant Pasture, by the
Pipe of a Highland Orpheus'. Cattle sales
were undoubtedly held here, and many
cattle, after being nourished by the sweet
grass of this district, were driven to the

expanding industrial towns as good beef 'or
the hoof'.

Follow the track towards Middle House
which is one of the farmsteads improved b
Walter Morrison, a wealthy Victoria
landowner who summered here, spendin
the winter at his London home. The ol
Middle House, situated about a quarter o
a mile away, has just been restored by th
National Trust, who own the estate.

Look out for a wooden sign on the lef
indicating a bridleway. This begins at a
point a little further north where, just of
the track on the left, a wire fence i
provided with a stile near a signpost wit
three fingers. One 'finger' directs th
walker to Street Gate, another is marke
'BW Arncliffe 3½' and the third arm
(which you will follow) is for 'Malham Tarr
¼ mile'. This route is known as the Monks
Road and, while using it, you might try t
imagine the men connected with th
religious houses and their servant
travelling hither and thither on monasti
business.

Make for a gate in a wire fence; just to
the left of the gate is a step-stile, givin
entry to another large pasture. The walke
eventually has a splendid view of the tarn in
its saucer-like depression; it is relativel
shallow, being no more than fourteen fee
(4.2m) deep.

Charles Kingsley, a friend of Walte
Morrison, fished for trout and developed
while visiting this limestone country, som
of the ideas he elaborated in his famou
book *The Water-Babies*, dealing with th
adventures of Tom the chimney sweep
Walter Morrison told visitors:

'The mansion down one of whose flues
little Tom came into little Ellie's room, was
doubtless Hovington House. Thence
Kingsley came on hither, found that we
used the Itchen flies, but much larger and
went on writing *The Water-Babies*.

Malham Moor was formerly part of the estate of Fountains Abbey.

"Vendale" is Littondale, with bits of the Yoredale rocks, etc., from Ingleborough thrown in; while "Lowthwaite Crag" is Malham Cove, whereon you can see the black mark made by little Tom as he slipped down it in a state of profuse perspiration.'

Turn right to follow the unmetalled road in a wooded setting to Malham Tarn House, now used as a field centre. When this house was badly damaged by fire in April 1873, the owner, Walter Morrison, lost no time in rebuilding. At this time, the entrance front and an Italianate bell-tower were added. The top of the tower was dismantled around 1963. The construction work was carried out with fine sandstone ashlar. To the south front was added a verandah, with cast iron columns springing from stone pedestals to support a glazed canopy.

West of the house, a road traverses a rock cutting and, just beyond, is a splendid new feature of the estate: a path – well shielded from waterfowl – leading down to a hide by the water, from which visitors can watch the birds and beasts of the area without being seen by them. During its first year of operation in 1991, a pair of coot helpfully nested on a branch protruding from the water a few yards from the hide.

Return to the house and retrace your steps through the wooded area to where the road is close to the tarn. Notice that many trees are growing behind circular drystone walls, where they are safe from browsing sheep. Pass through a gate, and then leave the unmetalled track (right) for a grass track bearing right and leading to the car park at Tarn Foot.

WALK 17: STAINFORTH TO FOUNTAINS FELL

Start: Stainforth Car Park. Grid Ref: 821 673
Distance: 12½ miles (20km)
OS Map: Outdoor Leisure 10
Walking Time: A steady day's walk

Climbing on to the peat and heather ridge of Fountains Fell at 2,192 feet (668m) makes a fascinating excursion. With only one footpath, the Pennine Way, over an immense area, and the need for a circular walk, this is the 'big one' in this book. It slightly overlaps walk 13. No special problems are envisaged, but good boots and stamina are necessary. Fountains Fell is so often swathed in cloud that a compass is a useful accessory. Stainforth, on B6479 north of Settle, has an unattended car park at which the motorist is trusted to pay his dues.

The Ribble Way does not stick slavishly to the banks of the river. Between Stainforth and Helwith Bridge is a footpathless gorge, in which the railway engineers built a magnificent viaduct of dressed stone, contriving that it should have a ruling gradient of 1 in 100 and also be on the 'skew', its large piers positioned to offer least resistance to the rush of water.

Walkers on the Ribble Way, having left the riverside at Stainforth Bridge, take a hill walk from the village. Motorists use a car park with an 'honesty box' for parking fees. Seek out the church, near which is Stainforth House. To the right of this large building is a footpath sign bearing the emblem of the Ribble Way and indicating 'Moor Head Lane 1½'.

The path goes uphill, using stiles and passing to the right of a field barn. In a field where a beck with waterfalls provides an attractive feature, do not cross the beck. Maintain the steady climb to where the path crosses an area of rushes and has been waymarked with yellow-painted posts. Being on the Ribble Way ensures that this part of the walk is well-defined.

A panoramic view includes Penyghent, Fountains Fell, Pendle Hill (just inside Lancashire), Whelpstone Crag, Smearsett, Ingleborough and Whernside.

A stile gives access to Moor Head Lane and immediately across the track is a fingerpost, 'Long Lane 1¾', the path going diagonally to run along a wallside. The views westwards include the quarries of North Ribblesdale, the limestone cliffs at Beecroft, Horton-in-Ribblesdale and dark Silurian terracing near Helwith Bridge, where an older slate quarry, now flooded, is in clear view.

A stile leads over a wall and a fingerpost indicates 'Churn Milk Hole ½'. Turn right for Dale Head and a metalled road (Stainforth-Halton Gill).

Ulfkil Cross, a monastic marker, was a rallying point for those of the far-flung parish of Giggleswick who supported the Pilgrimage of Grace, a sixteenth century uprising in support of the monasteries threatened with dissolution. The cross base, which stood beside the road near the cattle grid, has been moved to a position just inside a nearby field.

Walk for a short distance along the road to where the wire fence (right) may be crossed by a simple little wooden stile. In the large pasture beyond, do not wander too far from the line of the road. Where there is a barn at the roadside, let your eye trace the wall (right) to a corner with a stile leading to tussocky ground, which in

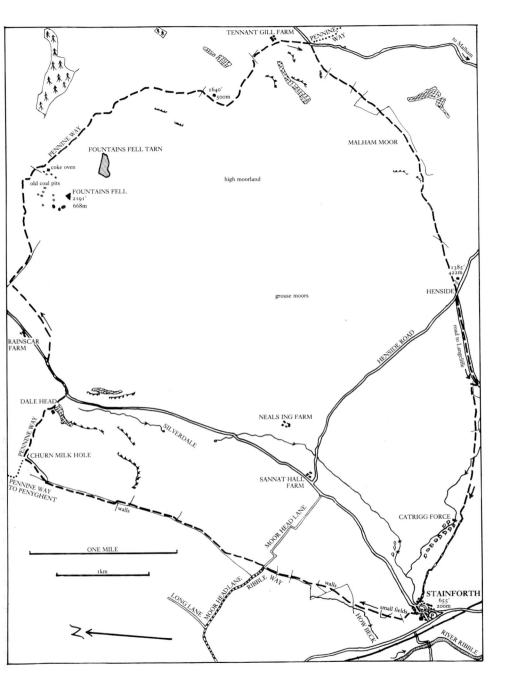

TENNANT GILL FARM

PENNINE WAY

to Malham

1640'
500m

MALHAM MOOR

PENNINE WAY

FOUNTAINS FELL TARN

coke oven

old coal pits

FOUNTAINS FELL
2191'
668m

high moorland

grouse moors

1385'
422m

HENSIDE

RAINSCAR
FARM

HENSIDE ROAD

road to Langcliffe

DALE HEAD

PENNINE WAY

SILVERDALE

NEALS ING FARM

CHURN MILK HOLE

PENNINE WAY
TO PENYGHENT

SANNAT HALL
FARM

CATRIGG FORCE

walls

MOOR HEAD LANE

ONE MILE

1 km

LONG LANE

MOOR HEAD LANE

RIBBLE WAY

walls

small fields

STAINFORTH
655'
200m

HOW BECK

RIVER RIBBLE

Penyghent and Ingleborough, from Fountains Fell.

summer is white with the downy heads of cotton grass.

The view northwards is of Rainscar Farm, backed by the immense form of Penyghent, which is so dominant it can be seen in clear weather from the bridge at Settle. Daniel Defoe in 1724 saw 'nothing, but high mountains, which had a terrible aspect ... especially Penigent Hill'. William Paley (1743-1805), who had an enormous intellect, was one day seen meditating while standing on Settle Bridge.

When someone inquired what he was thinking about, Paley gave the surprising reply: 'I was just thinking how like Penyghent is to a raised pie'.

Fair weather views take in the fells of Littondale. The walker has an occasional glimpse of the western slope of Fountains Fell. The Pennine Way passes through an area of peat, and a step stile gives easy access over a wall to the old Coal Road. Turn right for Fountains Fell.

Initially, the ground is moist enough to

Marsh marigold.

hold marsh marigolds. Cross a prominent band of floriferous limestone, before bearing left along a well-defined raised track. A farm – the only habitation in view to the west – is Penyghent House, beside the road to Halton Gill. The farm is on the rim of Penyghent Gill, which also descends to Littondale.

Birds to be seen over the rushy ground below the Coal Road include skylark and meadow pipit. The short-eared owl, a diurnal owl, crosses the moor like a large brown moth, looking for small mammals as food for its young. These hatch in a ground nest, but soon spread out and remain still and silent when the adults signal danger. This dispersal undoubtedly has a survival value if there is a marauding fox. With luck, the predator finds only one bird.

Fountains Fell's upper rocks are of gritstone, with ledges packed with peat and bilberry. The way lies across a small beck and continues on a well-pounded track which meanders, with a cairn or two as markers, to a recently rebuilt wall which incorporates concrete slabs as steps.

The felltop is broad, chocolate-brown and moist with peat, lagged by coarse grasses, some heather, much bilberry and also cloudberry. Gritstone is everywhere, having been used for innumerable decorative cairns, and areas fenced off with light wooden barriers must be approached with great care, marking the location of the relatively deep pits of the old Fountains Fell Colliery. There is also, on the felltop, a squat building that many suppose is a shelter for sheep. In reality it is a coke oven, dating from about 1810.

The colliery's production during its few years of existence was 900-1,000 tons of coal per annum. The coal, intended for industrial use, was removed by packhorses to Malham Smelt Mill (1815-1910), of which only a restored chimney remains. The coke made from Fountains Fell coal was used for calamine from the Pikedaw Mine. The calamine was roasted before delivery to the brass-founders.

Coal, as opposed to coke, was delivered to the lime-burners who had congregated in the vicinity of Buckhaw Brow, north of Settle. Brayshaw and Robinson, in their history of Giggleswick parish, mentioned the coal's impurity. It gave off noxious gases. A lime-burner, lying unconscious by his kiln, was saved from death by the chance arrival of a customer.

Fountains Fell has a stock of red grouse, the hardy 'moorcock'. As such, it has given a name to many a Pennine hostelry. Bird visitors for nesting include the golden plover and dunlin, the latter frequenting the edge of a large tarn to feed.

The Pennine Way does not cross the summit of Fountains Fell but slips quietly off the high ground, its surface alternating between firm ground and areas of black peat. Northwards, the wild lands slope down to Darnbrook, one of the big sheep farms of Malham Moor, which is recalled by motorists because here a gate extends over the road and, beyond, the road climbs steeply with formidable bends.

The path from Fountains Fell to Tennant Gill loses height gradually. Away to the south, a clear weather view includes Malham Tarn. A wall is crossed by step stile. A notice announces entry into the Malham Tarn Estate of the National Trust, and the path descends beside a broken-down limestone wall towards the old sheep farm of Tennant Gill. The path bears left to a stile beside a gate. Continue the downward progress to pass at the edge of the group of farm buildings. Follow the lane to the metalled road (Malham-Arncliffe), but do not cross the road. A fingerpost marked 'Henside' is the route to take. Like the crossing of Fountains Fell, it is a featureless route in poor weather. The big pastures have tufts of rush and swallow holes.

The footpath reaches a road where there is a T-junction, the stem of the 'T' being the road to Langcliffe via the farmstead at Cowside. The placename element 'side' is usually derived from *saetr*, the summer grazing area of the farmstock in Norse days. The path leads down a shallow valley to Catrigg Foss and Stainforth.

WALK 18: GORDALE SCAR, WATER SINKS AND MALHAM COVE

Start: Malham, National Park Centre Car Park. Grid Ref: 900 626
Distance: 6 miles (9½ km)
OS Map: Outdoor Leisure 10
Walking Time: 3½ hours

Memories of this Malham tour, taking in Gordale Scar and Malham Cove, will endure. At Gordale, water continues to enlarge a shadowy chasm in which the cliffs overhang dramatically, and the beck appears from an eye-hole in the rock and seethes down a boulder slope. An alternative path to the stiff climb by the waterfall in Gordale is given. Malham is reached from the A65 between Skipton and Settle by one of several roads. That via Gargrave and Eshton is in a park-like setting, and the high road from Settle to Kirkby Malham offers panoramic views in clear weather.

Malham is one of the 'honeypots' of the Dales, attracting a million people a year. A guide of 1886 mentioned Malham's remoteness from railway stations – five miles from Bell Busk, seven from Hellifield and six from Settle, adding 'it is a toilsome walk over the hills from Settle, and difficult to find'.

The head of Malhamdale might look austere, but the village has a cosy position beside the beck which flows from the base of Malham Cove. That beck once divided the lands belonging to two great abbeys, Fountains property being on the west and Bolton's on the east.

In the eighteenth century, the first tourists – people of 'taste and leisure' – were attracted to Malham by the limestone splendours such as the cove and Gordale Scar. In 1807, William and Dorothy Wordsworth 'rested under the huge rock [of Gordale] for several hours, and drank of its cold waters'.

The Yorkshire Dales National Park has an information centre featuring the history and traditions of Malhamdale; there is also a goodly array of books and leaflets.

Birds are thinly spread, though house martins (the swallow-like birds with shorter tails and white rumps) plaster their mud-and-straw nests on the overhangs of Malham Cove, and the dipper – a lively bird of unpolluted hill becks – is frequently seen, being fiercely territorial.

Plants abound in areas which have not been over-grazed by sheep. Some of the first flowers of the year have a yellow hue, two examples being the bulbous buttercup (the sepals are turned back) and birdsfoot trefoil (a creeping plant with pea-shaped flowers). Fairy flax sports tiny white flowers, and the summer's offerings include the blues of scabious and harebell.

The path to Janet's Foss and Gordale Scar is reached from the information centre by crossing the road, then the beck (using a small bridge or stepping stones). Go right. Signposts direct you to the little gorge, decked by ash and hazel, where Janet's Foss tumbles into a clear, cold plunge pool.

A rookery is a noisy feature in springtime. Such is the clarity of the water in the beck that anyone sitting quietly above the fall might see a dipper underwater, working the bed of the stream for larvae and other titbits. The humid atmosphere of this locality is ideal for mosses and ferns. In April and May, the hooded flowers of the cuckoo pint are conspicuous; they develop

The impressive limestone entrance to Gordale Scar.

into spikes with scarlet berries. The woodland floor, in spring, is whitened by wild garlic. A loud, hard call emanates from the throatbox of the wren, which looks far too small a bird to be able to offer such a rousing call.

Foss is a Norse word for waterfall, and Janet (or Jennet) is said to have been the queen of the local fairies. She lived in the (far from comfortable) quarters of a cave behind the waterfall. The fan of white water was created when a limestone bedrock was dissolved and eroded by the action of water, and then redeposited on

mosses growing at the lip of the waterfall as a fragile screen of a substance known as tufa.

Each June, farmers washed their sheep in the pool beneath the waterfall. This process, undertaken just before clipping time, removed from the fleeces any grit picked up by the sheep. It also removed the last traces of salve, a mixture of butter and tar applied to the skin the previous November in the belief that salved sheep wintered better than the others.

The old bridge between Janet's Foss and Gordale Scar has been closed to traffic, a new one being provided. The water flows through large pipes. Make a mental note of the signpost 'Malham Cove' beside the old bridge, for this marks the path that will eventually be taken by those who do not wish to climb the waterfall in Gordale Scar.

The path to Gordale Scar is spread with 'quarry bottoms' (small stuff), giving it a durable and dazzlingly white appearance. Watercress thrives in the clear beck. Jackdaws utter their short, sharp calls when disturbed; they nest in cracks and crannies.

Gordale Scar, on the line of the Mid-Craven Fault, was described as 'a collapsed cave' by many writers, but is believed to have been created simply by a furious rush of water as vast quantites of ice melted at the end of the glacial period. Within the gorge, the 160 feet (50m) high cliffs soar and protrude grandly at the top, at one point coming within 50 feet (15m) of each other.

Early travellers were awestruck at Gordale. The poet Thomas Gray watched with amazement in 1769 as some goats frolicked on the cliffs, and added that 'one of them danced and scratched an ear with its hind foot in a place where I would not have stood still for all the world'. The Rev John Hutton of Kendal, in his *Tour of the Caves* (c1780), took up Gray's theme of adventurous goats, noting that 'some goats frisked about with seemingly wanton carelessness, on the brink of this dreadful precipice, where none of us would have stood for all the pleasant vales washed by the River Aire'.

James Ward's immense painting of Gordale, which he completed in 1815, now hangs in the Tate Gallery. Ward pleased his patron, Lord Ribblesdale of Gisburn Park, and provided a stimulus for tourism, when he included some romantic touches: a white bull and two stags, the antlers of the deer being locked in combat.

The void of Gordale is usually in

The 240 feet high Malham Cove.

shadow. Not until the midsummer sun works its way round is the gorge fully lit up, though, on bright days, good photographs can be obtained of the beck as it makes its foaming descent, spilling over tufa, the substance already seen at Janet's Foss.

A notice warns that care should be taken, and that the climb up by the waterfall is difficult. Those who wish to avoid this stretch should return to the sign by the old bridge, and follow the path by Cawden and subsequently the Pennine Way north to Tarn Foot.

Above the lower falls in Gordale Scar, the path is steep and rocky. Yellow arrows on the rock direct walkers towards the left, and eventually there is a climb on steps composed of baulks of timber with in-filling above each. Stop now and again and look around in this damp, grey world.

The ascent is short and sharp; the walk continues over almost level ground, on close-cropped turf lying between limestone pavements. Stiles, cairns composed of limestone rocks and some very short posts

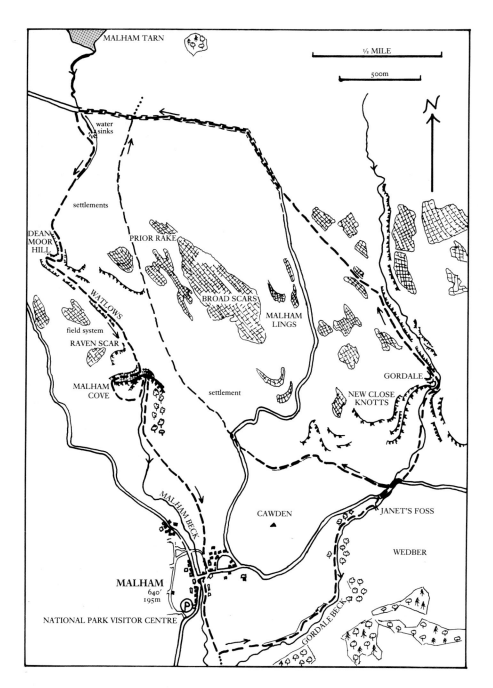

MALHAM TARN

½ MILE

500m

N

water
sinks

settlements

DEAN
MOOR
HILL

PRIOR RAKE

WATLOWS

BROAD SCARS

MALHAM
LINGS

field system

RAVEN SCAR

MALHAM
COVE

settlement

GORDALE

NEW CLOSE
KNOTTS

MALHAM BECK

CAWDEN

JANET'S FOSS

WEDBER

MALHAM
640′
195m

NATIONAL PARK VISITOR CENTRE

GORDALE BECK

mark the way to the road. The wall is negotiated by a good old-fashioned stile with protruding stones. Bear right to follow the road, which turns left for Tarn Foot.

Just beyond where the beck from Malham Tarn flows under the road, use the gate (left) for access to land where the beck – disappears! Notice how the flow of water is normal – then seeps into the ground. The explanation is that at what has become known as Water Sinks the stream has crossed a geological fault, passing from the impervious slate on to limestone. Subsequently it flows underground to reappear in the dale below Malham.

Walk with a limestone wall on your left. The rocky path (highly polished by boots, and inclined to be slippery in either dry or wet weather) begins its descent to the dry valley known as Watlowes, where – as in Gordale Scar – there was once a raging torrent.

A stile leads on to Ewe Moor, which is mentioned on a plaque erected by the owners, the National Trust. Soon your boots will encounter the limestone pavement above the cove. Ash trees grow from the face of the sheer cliff, and jackdaws are often in noisy flight. On good days, climbers on the rock walls resemble multi-coloured spiders.

The cove, a spectacular feature on the Mid Craven Fault, at the southern limit of the Great Scar limestone, is 240 feet (73m) high. After the Ice Age, the overflow from the tarn flowed over the cove, eroding it back to form a curved crag. Water issuing from the foot of the cove as Malham Beck originated at a water sink near the old smelt mill chimney on the moor.

The pavement, with its limestone blocks known as clints and the deep channels called grikes, was eroded over the space of thousands of years. Limestone which had been scraped clean by ice was now dissolved by slightly acidic rainwater. The rounded channels on some clints suggest that these partly developed under soil.

The grikes vary greatly in depth, but almost all of them have been colonised by plants. Dog's mercury is to be found almost everywhere, its green flowers being without petals. Hart's tongue fern is easily recognised because of its broad fleshy fronds. Herb robert, with its bright pink flowers, is another colonist of the limestone pavement. Wall rue sports tiny leaves which are divided into fan-shaped sections. Of the spleenworts, maidenhair is conspicuous with its small ladder-like leaves, the stalk and midrib being black.

In the vicinity of the cove, and extending down to the beck, are the remains of Iron Age field systems, their outline indicated by faint banks which show up best in evening light or after a light snowfall. The pattern of drystone walls has great appeal to visitors. However, in the 1850s, when the enclosure walls were still new, a visitor called William Howson mentioned their tedious uniformity!

The valley below Malham Cove is reached by crossing a stile (actually two stiles, side by side) and undertaking a knee-jarring descent over large steps to the level of the beck. Walk to the foot of the cove before returning to Malham by 'the great white way' (made up of more quarry waste).

A recommended variation from the popular route back to the village is to cross a clapper bridge (made up of slatey slabs) and head for 'Bombey's Barn' (as marked on a direction sign). The track goes to the right, climbing a shallow gradient to the barn (ruined) and continuing along a hard track to where it enters a narrow lane between limestone walls.

This is an impressive stonescape, with heaps of rock dumped by the original wall-builders and walls flanking the lane that descends to Malham, passing near to the youth hostel.

WALK 19: HANLITH, WEETS TOP AND THE UPPER AIRE

Start:	Kirkby Malham. Grid Ref: 894 610
Distance:	6½ miles (10½ km)
OS Map:	Outdoor Leisure 10
Walking Time:	4½ hours

A few discriminating walkers are seen on the moorland 'trod' between Hanlith and Weets. The route includes a descent to Janet's Foss on a little-used road and a not-too-demanding walk east of the River Aire. Although the circuit is joined at Hanlith, Kirkby Malham is chosen as the starting point because of the appeal of its historic church. Parking is usually available nearby.

Kirkby Malham Church is dedicated to St Michael the Archangel, the subject of a modern effigy in a niche on the porch. It is a building on the grand scale and has been called 'the cathedral of the Dales'. The immense tower is visible from hills around the dale.

A church is mentioned in the *Domesday Book*. The first legal reference to it occurs in a charter of confirmation by King John to the Abbot and Canons of West Dereham, Norfolk, in 1199.

General John Lambert, of Civil War fame, was born at Calton Hall in the parish in 1619. His birthplace was destroyed by fire during the lifetime of his son, and the present hall is in a plainer style. Local historians used to argue about the authenticity of the signature 'Oliver Cromwell' in the church register for 1655, when he is said to have been witness at a marriage. The Victorian historian Speight states that at this time Cromwell was visiting Lambert at Calton. That page from the register has disappeared.

Walter Morrison, of Malham Tarn House, paid for a thorough restoration of the church in 1879, and his grave, marked by a slab of stone with a simple inscription, is in the capacious graveyard.

The verges of a quiet road to Hanlith (meaning 'the hill-slope of Hagena') are, like others in the dales, linear nature reserves. Verge-trimming does not take place until the plants have set their seed. In spring, the pink spikes of butterbur appear before the rhubarb-like leaves, which eventually smother their selected areas. Other common plant species are lesser celandine, ground ivy, herb robert and shining cranesbill.

Pied wagtails are seen on the walls, where nesting takes place. In this area, the austere upper dale is giving way to one that is park-like in appearance. Curlews glide and call over a landscape distinguished by mature sycamores and velvety sward.

Ignore the riverside path to Malham; instead, cross the bridge and walk uphill near the stylish Hanlith Hall, which has been remodelled three times, the original building being erected in 1668 by the Serjeantson family, who used the outline of a halberd as an emblem. The front of the present hall was commissioned by the Illingworths and constructed shortly before the First World War.

The road winds, gaining elevation, and passes a verge where the plants include sweet cicely, which, tall and thick-stemmed, and with a mass of white flowers that looks like froth from a distance, has an aniseed scent, as you will discover on crushing and smelling a leaf. Wood cranesbill grows hereabouts and the colour can vary from mauve to a dark purple,

Sweet cicely is a member of the carrot family.

though it never attains the deep blue of the meadow cranesbill which grows profusely on local roadsides.

The walker in Malhamdale may see solomon's seal, with its angled stem and flowers like a row of small white, green-tipped bells. Common roadside plants include cow parsley, knapweed (with purple flowerheads), sheep sorrel and lady's mantle (lobed leaves and pale green flowers).

The road merges with the unmetalled Windy Pike Lane, the walls reflecting a change in the geology from limestone to gritstone. At the top of the hill, the view opens out spectacularly to reveal Malham village and beyond it the cove, Cawden Hill and Gordale Scar. Across the dale is Malhamdale School which serves the dale. The premises were the gift of Walter Morrison of Malham Tarn House.

Windy Pike Lane climbs steadily. Part of the small conifer wood on the left has been felled and re-planted, the young trees having plastic sleeves to protect them against mice or sheep which, being of the Swaledale breed, have dark faces and grey muzzles.

The lane ends at a field gate, beyond which stretches 'white' moor (containing coarse grasses, as as opposed to the peat and heather of the 'black' moor). Follow the route indicated by a signpost indicating 'The Weets'. The footpath, waymarked with yellow-topped posts, climbs in an area where views of upper Malhamdale are extensive. Beyond the dark line of larches, away to the north-west, is gleaming limestone.

The moorland 'trod' leads to a stile at a wall. Across this, and a boggy patch, is a multi-fingered signpost. The message to which you will respond is 'BW Weets Top ¼'. The white object against a wall ahead is a redundant triangulation station of the Ordnance Survey, who now use images from satellites when revising their maps.

At the next signpost, select 'BW Hawthorns Lane'. Go through the gate and stop to examine Weets Cross, the only known example locally of a monastic marker cross that has retained its stone shaft. Elsewhere only the bases remain. Long before the landscape acquired a pattern of drystone walls and roads, the great abbeys who had been granted land used stone crosses to mark the routes followed by their servants, and also to indicate the limits of their estates.

Follow Hawthorns Lane, left. In spring, cock lapwings flop about in the air, giving reedy calls, to impress the females. The lapwing calls shrilly when anyone goes too near its ground nest.

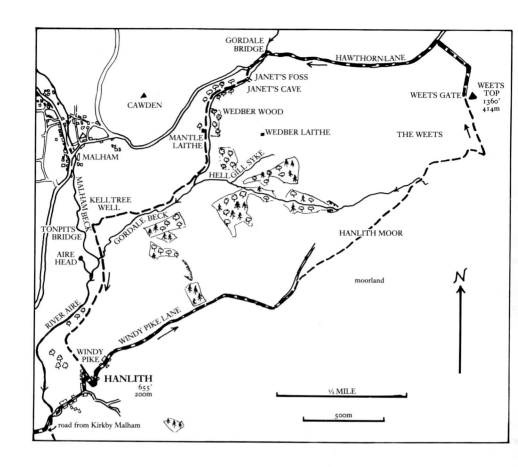

In view is Lee Gate Farm, with the hamlet of Bordley away to the right being partly hidden by a fold of the hill. Ignore the signpost 'FP Park House ½'. The lane to follow leads down to a metalled road (that from Malham to Lee Gate); turn left and go off down the hill to Gordale House. Notice, at the roadside near Gordale Farm and for some way beyond it, a profusion of butterbur by the beck and at the roadside. In view to the right is the approach to Gordale Scar.

Follow the beckside path from Janet's Foss to a point just south of Malham, where the Pennine Way is joined, leading south. At Aire Head, where two springs occur, the River Aire has its official source. Where the path climbs high, look down to see the river and the dam for Scalegill Mill. (Scalegill originally meant a hut by a small valley.) The vegetation beside the dam is lush, and here water birds like the coot – a dark bird with a white frontal patch to its head – may have seclusion when rearing their young.

Janet's Foss is said to be named after the queen of the local fairies.

A mill has stood on this site at least since the eleventh century, as it was mentioned in the *Domesday Book*. It has been used in turn for processing corn, wool, flax and cotton, and by the early nineteenth century it had become the major employer of labour at Kirkby Malham. A waterwheel was re-moved in 1929, when turbines were installed. Turbines are still in use for generating electricity. The premises have been converted into holiday cottages.

At Hanlith, follow the road back to Kirkby Malham.

WALK 20: KIRKBY MALHAM, SCOSTHROP AND KIRK SYKE

Start: Kirkby Malham. Grid Ref: 894 610
Distance: 5 miles (8 km)
OS Map: Outdoor Leisure 10
Walking Time: 3 hours

After the high hills and the huge vistas, it is pleasant to walk in a tidy small-scale landscape wher there is also a strong sense of history. Once again the parking place is Kirkby Malham, but this rout takes a southerly course, untimately crossing the Aire near Newfield Hall to return on the eastern bank There are parking places near the church.

The Angles founded most of the Malhamdale villages. In the seventh and eighth centuries they followed the rivers Aire and Wharfe up into the lower dales and settled at Malham, Hanlith, Airton and Calton. A century later, the Danes were here, occupying what is now Kirkby Malham and establishing a church which was doubtless built of wood and thatch. Its successor i that referred to as 'the cathedral of the Dales.'

This last walk in the series is south of the line between Hanlith and Kirkby Malham, where the valley offers lush grazing for farmstock and the mature trees give it a well-cared-for appearance.

Kirkby Malham Church, an excellent example of Perpendicular architecture.

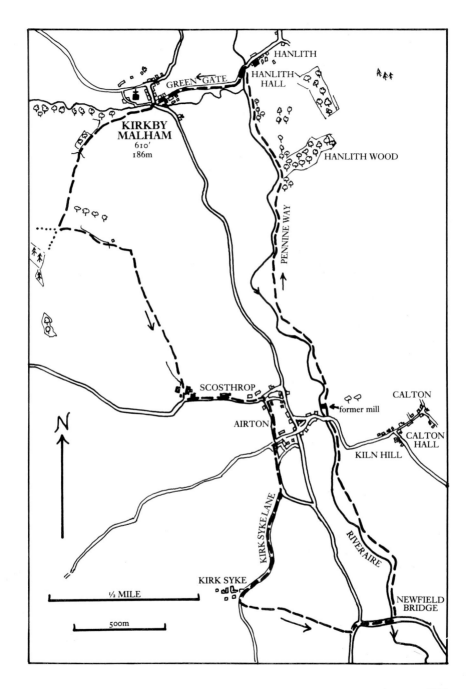

HANLITH

HANLITH
HALL

GREEN GATE

KIRKBY
MALHAM
610'
186m

HANLITH WOOD

PENNINE WAY

SCOSTHROP

CALTON

former mill

AIRTON

CALTON
HALL

KILN HILL

N

KIRK SYKE LANE

RIVER AIRE

KIRK SYKE

NEWFIELD
BRIDGE

½ MILE

500m

The snipe is most active in the mornings and evenings.

From near the church, cross Kirkby Beck by a wooden bridge and, using stiles, traverse the fields beyond. From these quiet fields are extensive views of Malhamdale. In the middle distance, just wide of Gargrave, is a detached group of hills dominated by Sharphaw, one of the 'beacon hills', the glow from a fire at the summit being seen at times of national emergency or rejoicing.

At a fingerpost, turn left for 'Airton', which is less than a mile away. It is fun locating the stiles. Eventually, you will find yourself in a large field with two modern farm buildings on the other side. The path to be followed lies between those two structures, to emerge on the Scotsthrop-Hellifield road.

Scosthrop lies cheek-by-jowl with Airton, the two townships having being separated by the width of a road since Norman times. The Anglian flavour endures at Airton in the way the old houses are grouped around a green, one house actually standing on it. Airton has a Friends' meeting house, built by a Quaker couple called William and Alice Ellis in 1700. Four years earlier, they had constructed a stone house for themselves; it is still known as Ellis House.

From Scosthrop, continue the walk by following a short stretch of bridleway which begins almost opposite the first of several wooden garages. The bridleway leads to the Airton-Hellifield road. Bear right, then almost immediately left (the signpost is for Bell Busk), and after about 200 yards (180m) bear right, a footpath sign indicating 'Bell Busk, 1½ miles'.

This bridleway also serves Kirk Syke Farm. It is a quiet, floriferous route. Where the verges are open, there grows a profusion of wayside flowers: meadow cranesbill, vetches, harebell, herb robert and giant bellflower.

Kirk Syke Farm has a name made up of *kirk* for a church and *syke*, a ditch or stream. Just beyond a shallow ford, a wooden stile (left) gives access to a field path to the road near a graceful bridge over the Aire, not far from Newfield Hall, which has latterly been used as a holiday centre.

Cross the bridge. On the left is a Pennine Way sign, with a subsidiary notice asking walkers to keep to the riverbank. There now begins a pleasant northward walk by the Aire to Hanlith Bridge.

In summer, the banks of the Aire are obscured by plants – butterbur, giant bell flower and masses of meadow cranesbill.

The birds are those you have come to expect in a Dales setting – dipper, curlew, lapwing, snipe, redshank and oyster-catcher, the latter a handsome pied bird sporting a long red bill.

The valley narrows at the approach to Airton, where an eighteenth century cotton mill by the river was rebuilt by the Dewhurst family about 1838. (The Dewhursts went on to build a mill on the grand scale at Skipton.) The old mill is no longer used by industry, having been divided into attractive living units. Wild rose grows in abundance beside the river just opposite this property.

Pass near some gnarled thorn trees. A thorn is a familiar sight in limestone country, especially the bare pavement areas, where quite often the thorns are stunted, taking on fantastic shapes and thus becoming 'characters', like the Dales farmers. In Yorkshire, *thorn* is a common placename element, as in Thornton-in-Lonsdale and Skyrethorns. Some impressive thorn trees must have existed when such villages were being named by early settlers.

The walker on the Pennine Way sees Hanlith Hall in a park-like setting long before the river bridge is reached. Cross the bridge and follow the road to Kirkby Malham, thus completing the circuit.

THE LONG DISTANCE WALKS

The Three Peaks   This walk is for those who are strong and well-equipped. The object is to reach the summit cairns of Penyghent, Whernside and Ingleborough within twelve hours, by a route chosen by the walker. Over the years, a Three Peaks circuit has become recognised, though not all of it is on official rights of way. The stretch is crossed by a few thousand peak-baggers annually.

The Three Peaks Walk involves a circuit of twenty-five miles (40 km) and a total of about 5,000 feet (1,500m) of ascent. Horton-in-Ribblesdale is recommended as the starting and finishing point. The wise walker 'clocks in' at the Penyghent Cafe and 'clocks out' at the end of the walk. Those completing the walk in less than twelve hours have a commemorative certificate posted to them by Peter Bayes, the public-spirited owner of the cafe.

On leaving the cafe, turn right, then almost immediately left to follow a lane marked 'Pennine Way'. Soon, a sign indicates 'Three Peaks route via Brackenbottom', necessitating a right turn. Having passed near a farmyard, go right, then almost immediately left over a wooden footbridge where there is a sign: 'Bracken-bottom and Penyghent'. Turn left.

At the edge of Brackenbottom, a sign indicates 'Footpath Penyghent 1⅝ miles'. Turn left. A stile into a field is the start of the climb to Penyghent, to the right of a wall which arches itself over an outcrop of limestone. A wooden walkway prevents further erosion in a peaty area. One and a half miles (2½ km) from Brackenbottom, a stile is crossed and a left turn reveals a view

of the formidable 'nose end' of Penyghent. The summit cairn has lost its shape. A double ladder stile spans the summit wall. Follow the direction indicated by the arm of the fingerpost marked 'Horton'. The slope has been much eroded by over-use. Lower down, where a durable path has been made, Three Peakers ignore the signpost marked 'Horton' and press on through an area without an official right of way. Initially, it is down a grassy slope. There follow several miles of peaty terrain. Extreme care is needed where the peaty ground looks wet. Two becks are crossed; walls are furnished with ladder stiles.

The Three Peaks route crosses the line of the Pennine Way and presses on to the north-west. Eventually, pleasanter lime-stone country is reached. The hard track between the farms of High Birkwith and Old Ing is crossed (see the notice: footpath, no cycling) on the way to Nether Lodge, thence to Lodge Hall and Ribblehead.

Just behind a clutch of road signs at the Ribblehead T-junction, you will see a sign for Whernside. The route keeps the railway on the left and crosses the line on a path beside an aqueduct, near the south portal of Blea Moor Tunnel. Initially, the path is paved with stones. The top of Force Gill (which is not on the route) has a splendid waterfall.

The path to the summit of Whernside is so eroded a walker can hardly miss it. It is also a wearying drag, relieved by sweeping views of a landscape which eventually embraces the tarns under Whernside. Ribblehead with its viaduct is prominent. The course of the railway can be traced as far as Rise Hill, beyond Dent.

At the summit, a squeezer stile gives access to the trig station. Return through the gap and continue along the footpath crossing the ridge, descending over broken ground, and eventually down a slope on

Competitors in the Three Peaks cyclo-cross negotiate a lane near Horton.

which great care must be taken because the wooden baulks used to form steps have been damaged by erosion.

The path descends to Bruntscar, where – as indicated by signs marked 'Hill Inn' – the walker turns right, then almost immediately left and follows the road across the valley to the main road. Turn left for the Old Hill Inn. The ascent of Ingleborough is described in walk 6.

To leave the plateau of this hill, return to the area from whence the final scramble began and take the path heading eastwards. It is a route which the Three Peaks Project has given a firm surface. A steady downward walk via an old shooting box leads to

Sulber Nick and takes an easterly course back to Horton.

The Pennine Way This 250 mile (400 km) route, from Edale in Derbyshire to Kirk Yetholm in Scotland, traverses Upper Malhamdale and crosses Penyghent. Britain's first long distance footpath has lost its distinction of being the longest, but remains a supreme test of fitness. Although it has been traversed in less than four days (by the runner or cyclo-cross enthusiast), the average walker takes about sixteen days to complete the route.

Anyone wishing to walk the section within the scope of this book might start at

Gargrave and head northwards on the bank of the River Aire to Malham. The route involves an ascent of the flight of steps beside Malham Cove and on to Malham Tarn, subsequently climbing Fountains Fell and Penyghent.

There follows a fifteen mile (24 km) stretch from Horton over Cam End and on to Hawes.

The Ordnance Survey's Landranger series is useful for Pennine Wayfarers, many of whom carry Alfred Wainwright's *A Pennine Way Companion*.

The Dales Way The Dales Way, of ninety miles (145 km) and taking some five days, connects Ilkley with Bowness-on-Windermere. It enters Three Peaks Country at Cam End and Gayle Beck, crossing the Settle-Carlisle railway on its way northwards to Dent.

The Ribble Way The Dales Way, with its origins in Wharfedale, merely flirts with the Three Peaks area, but the Ribble Way reaches the heartland. It is described as a seventy mile (110 km) recreational foot-path, and it keeps close to the banks of the Ribble from sea to source, which is surely the most satisfactory way of exploring a great river. The footpath enfolds through scenes of increasing grandeur.

The Ribble Way makes a triumphal progress up Ribblesdale, and at Gearstones it is recommended that the busy, unfenced B6255 is ignored in favour of a route to the west via Winshaw, High Gayle and a soggy area where the names include Black Rake and Dirty Gutter. Joining the Dent road, and turning right, the walker – now at 1,350 feet (410m) – has another 500 feet (150m) to ascend to the source of the Ribble. The approach is by a runnel named Jam Dike.

The Ribble Wayfarer looks for the highest of a number of springs – one that has never been known to dry up, even in a drought year, and which therefore gives the Ribble's main feeder a reliable start at an elevation of 1,800 feet (550m).

In addition to an official booklet about the way, obtainable in the locality, there is a guide of rather more than 100 pages written by Gladys Sellers and published by Cicerone Press.

SELECTED READING

General:

Marie Hartley and Joan Ingilby, *The Yorkshire Dales* (Dent, 1956; reprinted by Smith Settle, 1991). Detailing the life and traditions of each dale lying within the National Park.

Arthur Raistrick, *The Pennine Dales* (Eyre and Spottiswoode, 1968). Authentic and readable account of geology, prehistory and historical development.

Ordnance Survey Leisure Guide, *Yorkshire Dales* (AA and OS, 1985). A colourful compilation packed with useful or relevant information and including OS maps and suggestions for walks.

Geology:

David Crutchley, *Geology of the Three Peaks* (Dalesman, 1981). A general introduction, including a series of walks of prime interest.

Tony Waltham, *Yorkshire Dales: Limestone Country* (Constable, 1984). A compact guide of great value to walkers.

A Mitchell, *Yorkshire Caves and Potholes. No. 1. North Ribblesdale* (published by the author, Skipton 1937). An early popular review of its subject.

History:

Thomas Brayshaw and Ralph M Robinson, *A History of the Ancient Parish of Giggleswick* (Halton & Company, 1932). An indispensable historical review for anyone interested in the history of North Ribblesdale.

John Hutton, *A Tour to the Caves – in the environs of Ingleborough and Settle* (first published 1780; republished by S R Publishers, 1970).

Geoffrey Wright, *Roads and Trackways of the Yorkshire Dales* (Moorland Publishing, 1985). A well-researched study of the old routes.

Horton Local History Group, *Horton-in-Ribblesdale: the story of an upland parish* (North Craven Heritage Trust, Settle 1984). A succinct history of the upper dale, containing much that had previously not been recorded in print.

Natural History:

Joan E Duncan and R W Robson, *Pennine Flowers* (Dalesman, 1977). A general study of flowers of the uplands.

John R Mather, *The Birds of Yorkshire* (Croom Helm, 1986). A large survey which contains much of Dales interest.

W R Mitchell and R W Robson, *Pennine Birds* (Dalesman, 1985). Takes in the full length of the Pennines, but has much material about species.

Walking:

Gladys Sellers, *The Ribble Way* (Cicerone Press, 1985). Notes, maps and much practical information about the seventy mile long footpath.

INDEX

Illustrations are numbered in italics